CONSTRUCTING
A GARDEN

CONSTRUCTING A GARDEN

Planning • designing • building maintaining

COLLINS & BROWN

First published in Great Britain in 2001
by Collins & Brown Limited
London House
Great Eastern Wharf
Parkgate Road
London SW11 4NQ

1 3 5 7 9 8 6 4 2

British Library Cataloguing-in-Publication Data:
A catalogue record for this book
is available from the British Library.

ISBN 1-85585-605-0

A Berry Book, conceived, edited and designed by
Susan Berry for Collins & Brown Limited

Gardening Consultant: Joanna Chisholm
Editors: Alison Freegard, Jacqueline Jackson,
Amanda Lebentz, Hilary Mandleburg and Ginny Surtees
Editorial Assistant: Lisa Pendreigh

Senior Designer: Kevin Williams
Designers: Dave Crook, Claudine Meissner and Allan Mole
Design Consultant: Tim Foster
Art Director: Roger Bristow

Special photography: Howard Rice and George Taylor
Illustrations: Ian Sidaway
Garden designs: Tim Newbury
Planting plans: Yvonne Innes

Reproduction by Global Colour Ltd, Malaysia
Printed and bound in China by L.Rex Printing Co., Ltd.

CONTENTS

DESIGNING THE GARDEN

With a little know-how, it is possible to transform the most neglected or untidy plot into a garden that is as beautiful as it is practical. Designing a garden is about making the best of the space that you have. It involves organizing the various features and elements you wish to include in a cohesive, appealing way. But most important, it is about turning your garden into what you really want it to be. With designs for every shape and size of plot, it is easier than ever to become your own landscape gardener. You will find all the help you need to draw up your own plan and see it through to completion, including simple, step-by-step guides to adding features such as brick surfaces and paving, building steps and timber decks, and pagodas or fencing. With suggestions on what to plant and where, how to deal with problem areas, how best to disguise eyesores, lay lawns, make ponds and more, this section gives you the basic information to create a good-looking yet practical garden.

The need for design

To be successful, a garden has to both look good and be practical, too. The best way to realize these two aims is to start off with a design.

For every beautiful garden that has evolved without careful planning, there are many more that, despite considerable investments of time, effort and money, fail to work because they are either impractical or unattractive. This is because an unplanned garden is rather like a small house which is extended bit by bit, as and when the need arises. The resulting conglomeration of rooms and spaces is invariably never quite satisfactory either from the point of view of appearance or for practical purposes.

A garden design allows you to take all the features and elements you want to include and organize them in a harmonious way. You will effectively be combining a number of ideas that not only work well on their own but which will relate to one another in terms of both form and function. Proceeding with a design will at the same time give you the opportunity to check out the availability of the materials, ensure that they are suitable for your intended purpose and, of course, to ascertain their likely cost.

Another beneficial aspect of a well thought-out design is that it will enable you to build your garden in stages if you wish, in the knowledge that the end result will always be a coherent whole.

The scope and scale of your design will depend on the money and time available. Once you have a worked-out idea in place, you can zone the areas you wish to create (see p.13). It will pay to do the section closest to the house first.

Transforming a garden

The key to a successful transformation is to retain useful and important features, such as shade-giving trees or shrubs that screen a boundary, while incorporating new ones – for instance, a patio area near the house. To decide what to keep, you should take some time to assess the relative merits of each major element of the garden. It is a good idea to observe the garden for several months before making major changes, such as removing a tree that gives the site character. When planning where to sit and what to plant, note the incidence of sun and shade at different times of the day and in different seasons. Deciduous trees that cast heavy shade in summer can let in welcome light when leafless in winter.

A change of scene
The small, neglected and featureless garden (inset) has been given a facelift with a neatly shaped lawn, a paved patio near the house and well-ordered borders around the perimeter.

Basic design rules

The use of simple shapes and forms, whether two dimensional like flower beds and paved areas, or three dimensional structures such as pergolas and summerhouses, will not only make your garden design more effective, but will have the added benefit of making the garden easier and less expensive to build and look after subsequently.

In small gardens especially, it is easy to let a design run away with you and become overcomplicated in an effort to include all your requirements. Avoid falling into this trap by including in your garden only those features that have a high priority, such as a patio, lawn, outdoor storage and maybe a play area for the children.

Limit your choice of materials for paved areas to two or, at most, three different sorts. Similarly, structures such as fences, trellis, pergolas and the like, will all blend together much more successfully if they are built from the same material, whether it be timber, wrought iron or something else.

Resist the temptation to include many different varieties of plants and choose a few good structural plants instead. These will give the garden its shape even in winter, and should be supplemented by a limited range of other varieties planted in groups of three or five. This will be much more effective than using a wider range of plants all planted singly.

Informal plantsman's garden
A simple brick path and patio laid in a straightforward herringbone pattern create the 'holding' element for a diverse selection of shrubs and perennials.

Creating a theme

A single theme provides vital unity in a garden design. It can bring together and harmonize a mixture of features and ideas. Major themes can be based on a colour, on the use of a particular material, or on a geometric shape, form, or pattern.

Colour
Colour can be used in several ways. One is to make all the 'hard' elements (paving, walls, fences and so on) the same colour, or a combination of colours, such as warm grey with terracotta.

Another is to have a colour theme in the planting. This might be a single colour such as white or red (although this approach can be very restrictive, especially in a small garden) or perhaps a combination of complementary shades, such as pale yellow, soft pink and light blue. A third way would be to have a colour theme reflected in both the hard and soft elements.

Materials
This approach is most suited to the hard elements of a garden. For example you could build walls, patio, paths and raised beds using the same brick throughout, or maybe in a combination of brick and stone. Or you could make all the vertical structures such as fences and screens from the same wood, in one particular style – perhaps rustic.

Unity of shape, form and pattern
If you want to include materials and ideas that do not harmonize naturally, the use of a particular geometric shape can provide a theme. Two-dimensional elements, for example a patio, lawn or pool, can all be made circular or semi-circular. Extend this idea to the three-dimensional features, maybe using trees and shrubs that are naturally more or less spherical in shape, or that can be trained to be so, such as box or yew. Another approach might be simply to divide your garden into a series of equal squares or rectangles, each one fulfilling a different purpose – lawn, patio, kitchen garden and so on.

Formal patio
Minor changes of level and matched pairs of containers help to prevent a largely paved area from looking monotonous.

Introducing the third dimension

It is important when designing a garden to remember that it will be three-dimensional. The plants and structures that you mark out on your plan need to be thought of not only as occupying a certain amount of space on the ground, but also in terms of their height and density.

A weeping birch will produce a very different effect from, say, a conical evergreen, whereas an ornamental stone ball could be imitated by a ball of clipped box. The garden's basic framework – whether of living plants, man-made, or a combination of the two – gives the underlying structure of the three-dimensional effect,

and this can be greatly enhanced by the judicious use of vertical elements, such as arches, arbours, fences, walls and hedges, which form screening barriers or offer glimpses of what lies beyond.

In the garden plans on the following pages, as much thought has been given to these details as to the rest of the design. Boundary walls have been clothed with climbers, pergolas and arches beckon the onlooker into other parts of the garden, single specimen shrubs or trees act as focal points, and raised beds, steps and other features have been used to prevent large expanses of lawn or hard surfacing from looking flat.

Using vertical elements

By the careful selection and positioning of such verticals as fences, hedges, garden structures, trees and tall shrubs, it is possible to achieve a number of desirable effects in your garden.

Screening is useful for masking views of unsightly objects both within and outside the garden. Frequently, complete screening is almost impossible: however, planting just a tree or group of tall

shrubs to break up the outline of the unwanted view is often enough to have the desired effect.

Framing is the opposite of screening. Use it to draw

Enhancing a sloping garden

Three-dimensional elements accentuate the gentle slope of this garden: steps, the pergola and repeat planting of spiky, architectural foliage plants.

attention to a particular view within, or maybe outside, the garden, or to an object or focal point such as a statue or pond. While an arch is a classic example of a frame through which to look at an object or view, even the suggestion of an arch, for example the view between the trunks of two trees with mingling canopies, can be equally effective.

Both sun and shade are important and any reasonably sized vertical object, whether man-made or natural, can be

positioned to create sun-traps or areas of shade to suit.

Division of space is another key factor. Many gardens can be given an added dimension by subdividing them into smaller individual spaces. Often it is better to achieve this with objects such as tall shrubs than with walls or fences.

Screening buildings

Trellis and climbing plants together with leaf canopies afford privacy from the neighbouring block of flats.

The garden framework

Just as a building has a concrete or steel framework beneath its brick or glass facade, so a garden needs a framework or basic structure to build on. This framework can serve, if necessary, to break the garden down into different spaces according to the needs of the owner – for example to give an area for children's play, or an area for growing vegetables. Paradoxically, gardens that are subdivided into smaller areas often seem larger and more complex.

The framework can consist of man-made structures or plants, but is usually a combination of both, as the gardens on the following pages show.

Such a framework is necessary so that at any time of the year, particularly where the climate is temperate and many plants are deciduous, the essential shape of the garden is always present, even if only in a skeletal form. Without this, most gardens would appear flat and uninteresting, especially during the winter months.

Framework plants such as trees and large shrubs, both deciduous and evergreen, should be selected not only for their individual beauty but also for the way in which their scale and form act as foils to smaller flowering and foliage plants. Large evergreen shrubs and trees in particular are, by their nature, ideal for the purpose,

Organizing space
A raised trellis screen not only divides the garden, but with the rose-covered arch beyond and a meandering path, creates a vista down it.

even if their flowers are insignificant. Similarly, man-made structures, such as fences, trellises, pergolas and arbours, while having their own intrinsic attractions, must also be designed and detailed so that again, whatever the time of year, they will always be interesting.

Shrubs for framework
Neat, low-level hedges of clipped dwarf box (above) can firmly contain a wide variety of more exuberant plant forms.

Trees for framework
A group of Robinia pseudoacacia 'Frisia' forms a deciduous canopy over garden furniture, while an evergreen hedge provides a year-round backdrop.

Planning the garden

One of the most fascinating aspects of gardening is that every garden is unique, because every owner is also unique. This means that everyone's expectations of how a garden should be laid out to satisfy their own needs is going to be different from the next person's — sometimes only in the tiniest of ways, but at other times in major respects.

When looked at from the point of view of a single individual, planning a garden can be comparatively straightforward. If, for instance, you like growing vegetables, then the whole garden can be put down to vegetables! However, when a garden is going to be used by more than one individual, the choice of what goes in it, and where, suddenly becomes far more difficult and can often be quite challenging.

The first step in tackling the challenge is to draw up a list of what you (and perhaps other members of your family) want from the garden. Next you need to assess what you already have in terms of the garden's size and aspect and, in the case of an established garden, in terms of the plants and features that are already there. Finally, you will be ready to think about where to put the features you want, bearing in mind the need for ease of access around the garden and safety.

Existing garden plan
Make a sketch plan of your garden with any existing features. Decide which of these are worth retaining in the light of your list. Here, we could keep the mature cherry tree and the old concrete paving to use it to lay stone flags and build an arch.

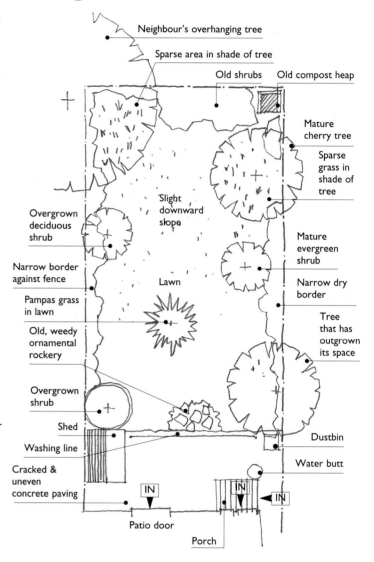

Your requirements

Make a list of your requirements in order of priority. The list here includes features for a family garden.

Be careful not to become involved with small details at this stage. Once the basic structure of the garden and the size, shape and position of major elements are established, then you can work out the detailing, such as plant varieties or the colour of the brick.

Utility
Line or rotary drier for washing
Paths
Shed for lawnmower, bicycles, tools
Screening for oil tank
Compost box
Lighting
Greenhouse
Higher boundaries
Bin store
Fuel store - coal, wood

Recreation
Patio or sitting area
   1 shaded, for summer
   2 sunny
Seating
Lawn

Play area
Water feature
Arch or pergola
Summerhouse
Ornaments/statues

Ornamental planting
Trees
Shrubs
Roses
Herbaceous border
Containers
Annual bed
Raised beds
Rockery/scree garden
Bog garden

Other planting
Fruit trees
Herb bed
Vegetable plot or area
Soft fruit cage

Safety
Safety, particularly in a garden used by children or old people, must be considered early in the planning stage. Steps should be regular (see p.33) and, if using a dark material, could be edged with lighter coloured material. Consider lighting them at night. If the garden is to include a play area for children, you could use wood or bark chippings as a surface (see p.40) to cushion falls. Avoid planting poisonous or potentially dangerous plants such as yew (*Taxus baccata*) and monkshood (*Aconitum*).

Assessing the space

There will be some things in your garden over which you have little or no control – its size, the direction it faces, the effect of neighbouring buildings or trees on the amount of sun or shade it receives, the presence of particularly damp or exposed spots, the type of soil. You will usually have to work with, not against these factors, so be prepared to make some compromises. It will help if you have prioritized your list of requirements.

With a small garden, for instance, the greenhouse might be low on the list, and if there were no space, it would have to go. However, a compromise might be to find room for a small cold or heated frame instead. Fruit trees, such as apples and pears, could be used in mixed borders in place of ornamental trees, while salad crops might be grown in spaces at the front of borders or in pots on the patio. Or, why not plant pergolas and trellises with climbing beans or a thornless blackberry which can be practical as well as attractive?

Finally, especially in a small garden, it pays to group all the utilitarian elements, such as the shed and bin store, in one place.

Zoning the garden
The plan of the garden with new areas dedicated to specific features, some features moved and removed, others added.

Focal point

Separation between utility and sitting area

Area catches late afternoon/early evening sun – alternative sitting

Utility area – shed, compost, storage etc.

Entrance to utility/ sitting area

Existing tree retained

Existing shrub removed

Ornamental area

Existing pampas removed

Existing evergreen shrub retained

Recreation area

Change of level

Feature – eg pool for foreground interest

Existing tree removed

Existing shrub removed

Shed moved to new position

Paving extended for sitting/recreation/ clothes drier/ bin storage

- - - - items moved or removed

Area for new conservatory

Porch removed

Access around the garden
The position and size of paths are essentially predetermined because they have to provide the links between different parts of the garden.

Especially important are the routes between the house and features such as a rear entrance, garage or tool store. The first priority in designing paths like these is to make them functional round-the-clock and all through the year. Other garden paths also need to provide safe, efficient access for foot traffic and wheelbarrows, but the way they are laid out depends on personal taste.

The design of paths and other surfaces, such as lawns, will considerably influence the appearance and feel of the garden. A regular, straight path gives a long, open vista, while a curving, informal path, partly hidden by planting, will suggest an air of mystery.

Remember, too, that a broad grass path or stretch of lawn invites a leisurely stroll, while a narrow, twisting path of diagonal brickwork will suggest a more hurried pace.

Angular pathways
Gravel paths meander slowly around the beds in this formal garden, inviting an unhurried pace and close inspection of the planting.

Drawing up the plan

So far you have been considering the garden in fairly general terms, working from sketch plans. Now is the time to measure the garden accurately and draw a scale plan of it. This will form the basis of your finished plan. With an accurate scale plan, you can start to finalize the location of your garden features. Remember that looks need to be combined with practicality. If you want a lawn for sunbathing, you will need to make sure it is located so that it receives enough sun. If a children's play area is required, it is not a good idea to put it in a far corner of the garden where the children cannot be watched over. The location of a patio, which ideally needs to be near the house for ease of access when entertaining, can be quite critical. If the area near the house is hot and sunny, a second sitting area in a shadier part of the garden may be worth considering. Also, to avoid glare on your patio, steer clear of light-coloured surface materials and gleaming white patio furniture.

Making a scale plan

A scale plan is simply an overhead view of the garden, reduced to a size that is convenient for you to copy onto a sheet of paper. Most plans are drawn to a scale of 1:50 or 1:100.

With a scale of 1:50, for example, every dimension you measure in the garden, such as the length of a fence, is divided by 50 before being drawn on the plan. Therefore, a 10m (30ft) long fence would be 20cm (8in) on the plan. Conversely, multiplying a dimension marked on the plan by 50, let us say a 6cm (2in) wide patio, will give you the patio's actual width – 3m (10ft).

Using this technique you can recreate the shape of your garden on paper, and then add the different features you want, all drawn to the same scale.

You should also add an indication of the garden's aspect – whether it faces north, south, east or west – as aspect can determine where some features should go.

Taking measurements
The arrowed lines give the dimensions you need to measure, including those of trees and shrubs to be retained. The diagonal measurement of the plot is necessary as your garden may not be exactly rectangular.

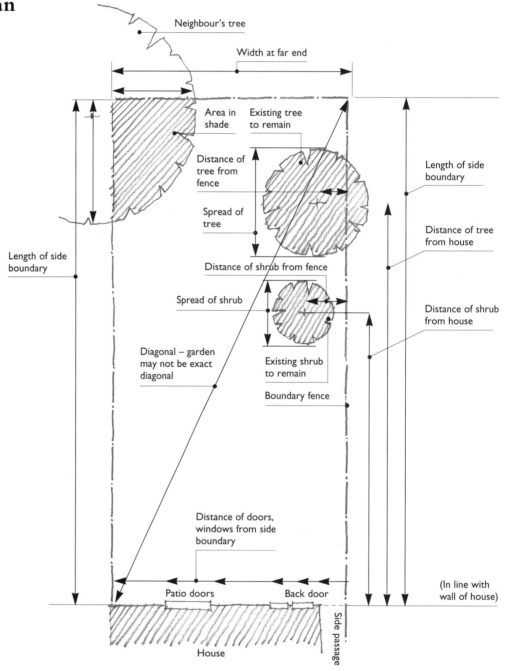

Neighbour's tree

Width at far end

Area in shade

Existing tree to remain

Distance of tree from fence

Spread of tree

Length of side boundary

Length of side boundary

Distance of tree from house

Distance of shrub from fence

Spread of shrub

Distance of shrub from house

Diagonal – garden may not be exact diagonal

Existing shrub to remain

Boundary fence

Distance of doors, windows from side boundary

Patio doors

Back door

(In line with wall of house)

House

Side passage

The finished plan

This plan of a family garden incorporates features listed on p.12. Needing relatively little maintenance, the result is both practical and good-looking. The large area of simply shaped lawn that almost reaches to the boundaries is much more practical than one or more small or oddly shaped areas, and is easier to mow.

The lawn is in the sunniest part of the garden and is connected to the patio to provide a useful overspill area for the occasional outdoor party or summer barbecue. There is a second, shaded area in the far corner, providing seclusion beneath the canopy of a neighbouring tree.

An alternative to the circular fountain in the ornamental gravel area might be a statue or sundial, a specimen shrub in a container, or perhaps a raised circular bed with planting.

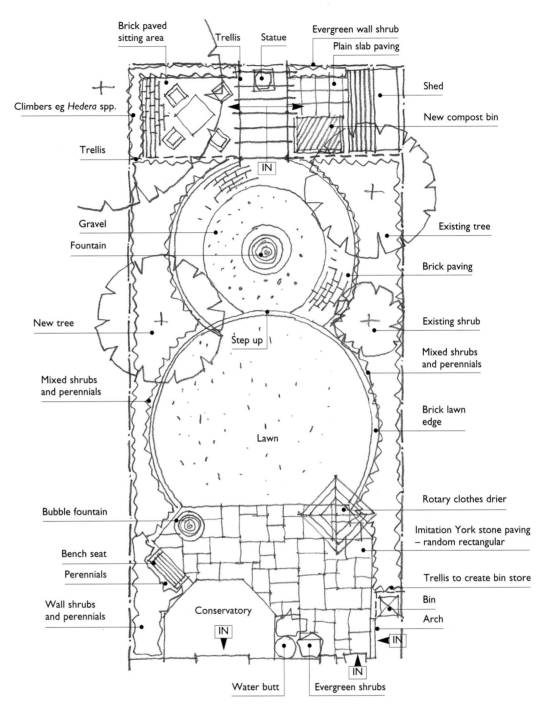

Estimating sizes

Measuring out sizes of features is an important element in design. To check that you have left enough space for a seating area, you should first check the patio is of a shape and size to accommodate your garden furniture and still leave room for people to walk around it.

Draw a rough sketch of your garden furniture set out as it usually would be, and seen from above. Mark its dimensions. This plan shows that the patio will need to be a minimum of 360 x 330cm (140 x 130in). These dimensions are based on a patio for a rectangular table and seating for six.

Use canes, pegs and string to mark out the various elements on the ground prior to construction. For marking out paths push a wheelbarrow along a 'path' of canes to see if it is wide enough and that it is possible to get round corners or sharp bends comfortably.

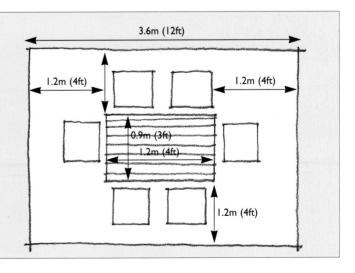

Constructing the garden

Having finalized your garden design, your next decision will be whether to carry out all or some of the work yourself, or whether to employ professionals. The advantages of doing it yourself are that it is less expensive, and you have complete control over all stages of the job. On the down side, you may find that you do not have enough free time to finish the work within your chosen time-scale, or that you do not possess all the necessary skills, particularly in specialized areas such as bricklaying. Even if you decide to pay for a professional, do not forget that you still need to take responsibility for ensuring that he or she is fully briefed and knows

what standards you expect. Whether you decide to use a professional or not, one of the advantages of having drawn up a plan is that it will enable you to phase the work. This obviously helps if you are doing it yourself, but it can also be useful if you are employing someone else as it will enable you to stagger the cost if you wish. Another factor you need to consider is the timing of the various stages of work. Certain seasons are more suited to certain jobs than others.

And finally, if you are doing the work yourself, you need to know how to deal with uneven ground, if necessary even terracing it.

Phasing the work

There are several different approaches to phasing the work. One that is useful for larger gardens is to identify a particular part of the garden and complete it in all respects from paving through to planting. The rest of the garden could then be put down to grass, used for vegetables or even kept bare. In year two a second area could be tackled and so on. Another option is to divide the work according to different elements or types of construction and complete several each year. In year one you might build the patio, paths and other hard landscape features such as a summerhouse base and a shed, and perhaps plant trees and a few shrubs that take a long time to mature. Year two could also see construction of a pergola or arch, a water feature, basic shrub planting and the completion of areas of grass. Finally, in year three, you could incorporate the finishing touches – ornaments, trellis, and climbers, a fountain in the pond and perhaps the summerhouse.

A three-year plan
This plan shows construction of the family garden (on p.18), with the work colour coded for each year. First priority is given to establishing permanent planting and laying hard surfaces near the house.
Year 1 (Brown)
Patio, path, shed, rotary clothes drier, trees, hedge around kitchen garden, climbers on fences and walls.
Year 2 (Green)
Lawn, play area, hedge around play area, mixed shrub border, shrubs to screen shed, prepare soil in kitchen garden, compost bin.
Year 3 (Red)
Bubble fountain, arch, climbers on arch, greenhouse, heathers/herbs/cut flower border, bin store, ornaments, pots and tubs, climbing frame etc in play area.

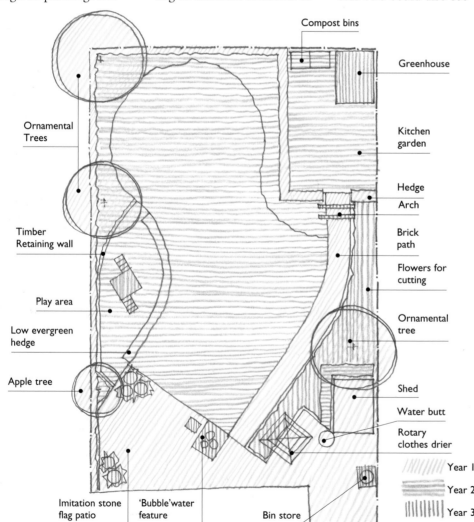

Compost bins
Greenhouse
Kitchen garden
Hedge
Arch
Brick path
Flowers for cutting
Ornamental tree
Shed
Water butt
Rotary clothes drier

Ornamental Trees
Timber Retaining wall
Play area
Low evergreen hedge
Apple tree
Imitation stone flag patio
'Bubble' water feature
Bin store

Year 1
Year 2
Year 3

Timing the work

Although most hard land-scaping can be carried out more or less all year round, it is particularly inadvisable to use wet concrete or mortars when the temperature is at or near freezing point, or when it is so hot as to dry them out rapidly. Also, if the ground is frozen solid then a lot of work becomes difficult or near impossible to carry out, so working during the depths of winter should be avoided.

Preparing the soil requires planning to achieve the best results. The ground should not be dug when it is frozen or so wet that the soil sticks to your boots and spade. If the soil contains either weed seeds or pieces of perennial weed root, these will need to be eliminated as far as possible

before planting. For this to happen, the weeds must first be visible so you can hoe or treat them in some other way, and the obvious time to do this is when they are active, between spring and autumn.

Heavy clay soils benefit from being roughly dug in the autumn and left to weather in winter frost and ice. You will then need to decide whether to plant next spring and risk weed infestation, or wait until the following autumn by which time you should have eradicated the weeds.

Planting is traditionally carried out between autumn and spring when most plants

Tackling major jobs

Avoid using wet concrete or mortar when the temperature is near, or at, freezing point, or if the conditions are very wet.

are dormant, that is to say not actively growing. The planting season can, however, be extended almost all year round where container-grown plants are used, as long as they are adequately watered, particularly during long, hot spells. Obtaining the plants for your garden

may require some planning, too. Once a nursery or garden centre has sold out of a particular line, it may not stock it again until the following spring or autumn. Advance ordering is therefore recommended if you do not want to have gaps in your borders.

Levelling uneven ground

There are occasions when, even with a seemingly flat garden, you will need to ensure that the ground is level – for instance when laying a lawn, patio or other area of paving. Similarly, if

you have a slightly sloping site, you will almost certainly want some level areas for lawn or sitting out. Alternatively, you may decide to add interest to such a site by making a

raised bed or terrace. Steep slopes are very difficult to manage without terracing, and may need professionally built retaining walls. It is often better to plan two small terraces rather than one big one. Unless you already have an abundance

of good topsoil, remember that when you excavate an area it is always worth conserving the topsoil for use elsewhere (for a lawn, for example). Store it in small heaps to prevent it from deteriorating through becoming compacted.

Excavating for terracing

Roughly mark out the area to be dug using canes, pegs and string. Then estimate the depth of the excavation. You will need pegs or stakes longer than this depth and a long straightedge and spirit level. If the straightedge is not long enough, you will need to use intermediate pegs as well.

Drive a peg into the ground at the top of the slope and a longer peg at the bottom, where your proposed terrace is to start. Lay a straightedge and spirit level between the two. Excavate the fall to depth 'A' (see right) to create a flat, even terrace.

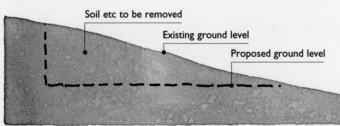

Marking out the ground
Mark out the area to be dug and estimate the depth of the excavation.

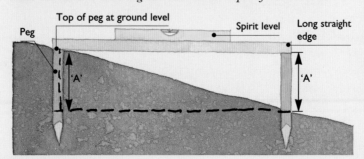

Positioning the pegs
Use a spirit level and straightedge to ensure the tops of the pegs are even.

Terraced garden
Raised beds, a seating area and summerhouse enhance this attractive, multi-level garden.

Family gardens

A family garden needs a design that will be compatible with a family's needs, while still making sure the garden looks good for as much of the year as possible. For families with small children, time is at a premium, so maintenance should be kept to a minimum. With children, open space is a priority, and so in each of these three designs the patio is generous and links directly to the lawn. In the rectangular garden, the patio extends into a paved utility area, with a shed, bin store and rotary clothes drier, all conveniently placed near the back door.

Year-round practicality
Mature shrub borders require relatively little maintenance to look good all year round. Here they successfully 'frame' an expanse of lawn which provides plenty of open space for energetic children.

The rectangular garden

A small kitchen garden with greenhouse is in the far corner, diagonally opposite the patio. This arrangement allows more space for the lawn and makes the garden appear larger. A brick path provides a practical, all-weather link between the house and kitchen garden and contrasts in colour and style with the square flags of the patio and utility area.

In addition to the generous lawn and patio, there is a separate play area for small children which is ideally located for supervision from the house or elsewhere in the garden. A bubble water feature makes a focal point at the corner of the patio, and acts as a divider between the patio and the utility area. At the far end of the gently curving path, a rustic arch makes an attractive feature and marks the entrance to the kitchen garden.

The planting consists of trees, shrubs and perennials, carefully selected to give year round interest with minimum work, and including varieties that can be used for cut or dried flowers. There is also a small herb bed situated in the sun, with convenient access to the kitchen.

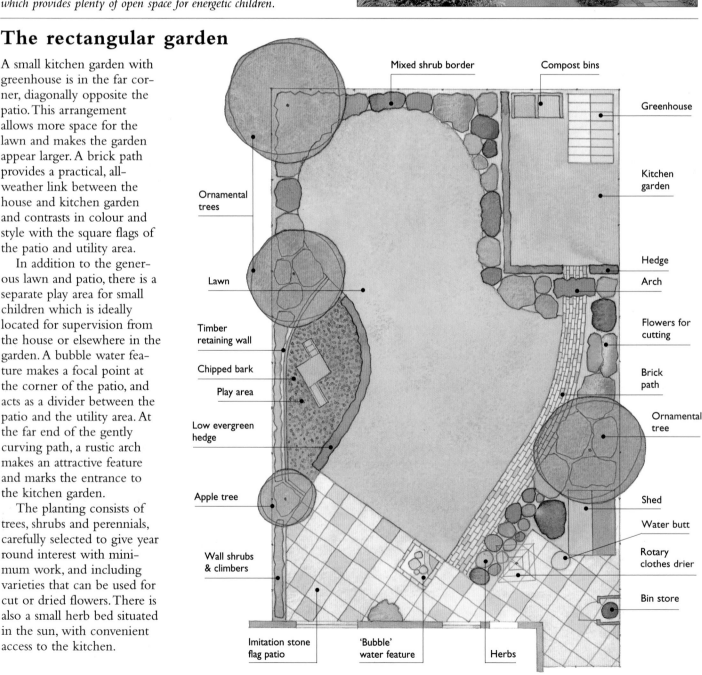

Mixed shrub border

Compost bins

Greenhouse

Kitchen garden

Ornamental trees

Hedge

Lawn

Arch

Timber retaining wall

Flowers for cutting

Chipped bark

Brick path

Play area

Low evergreen hedge

Ornamental tree

Apple tree

Shed

Water butt

Wall shrubs & climbers

Rotary clothes drier

Bin store

Imitation stone flag patio

'Bubble' water feature

Herbs

Long narrow plot

Here, the relative positions of the key elements are more or less unchanged, but by placing the patio, path and kitchen garden at an angle, and dividing the lawn by a change in the direction of the path, the narrowness of the plot is effectively disguised.

Very narrow plot
On a long, narrow plot, you can grow vegetables, for example, on either side of the path rather than in conventional rows.

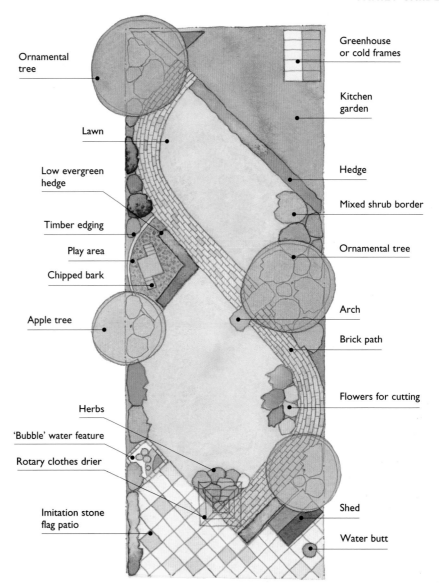

Ornamental tree
Lawn
Low evergreen hedge
Timber edging
Play area
Chipped bark
Apple tree
Herbs
'Bubble' water feature
Rotary clothes drier
Imitation stone flag patio

Greenhouse or cold frames
Kitchen garden
Hedge
Mixed shrub border
Ornamental tree
Arch
Brick path
Flowers for cutting
Shed
Water butt

Triangular plot

In this variation, the corners of the plot are taken up by the kitchen garden, screened from view by a hedge, and the play area surrounded with generous tree and shrub planting. This arrangement not only gets over the problem of narrow, awkward corners, but also maximizes the space available for the lawn and patio.

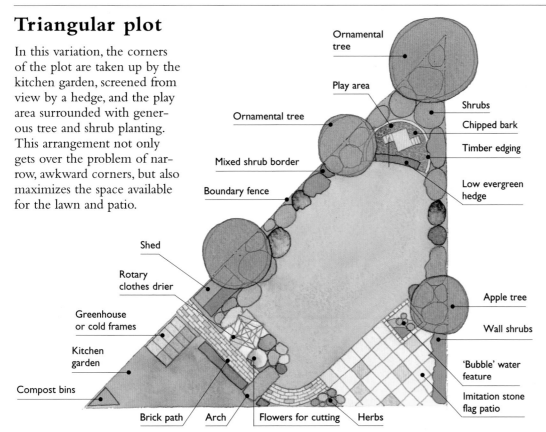

Ornamental tree
Play area
Ornamental tree
Mixed shrub border
Boundary fence
Shed
Rotary clothes drier
Greenhouse or cold frames
Kitchen garden
Compost bins
Brick path
Arch
Flowers for cutting
Herbs

Shrubs
Chipped bark
Timber edging
Low evergreen hedge
Apple tree
Wall shrubs
'Bubble' water feature
Imitation stone flag patio

Divisions in the garden
If the contours permit, a change of level between the patio and the rest of the garden helps to create a more 'private' feel to the sitting area.

Patio gardens

Enclosed by high walls or buildings, patio gardens can be small, angular, claustrophobic and bleak. But do not be deterred. There are many tricks to disguise these problems. Firstly, use planting to soften walls and disguise corners. With the boundaries partly concealed, the garden will appear larger. Secondly, any sense of squareness or angularity can be minimized by choosing a strong ground plan with a circular or curving theme, while any darkness may be overcome by painting the enclosing walls of the garden white, cream or another pale colour. On the plus side, patio gardens are relatively sheltered, so take advantage of this fact to grow more unusual and perhaps less hardy plants.

Secluded town courtyard
At the height of summer, a planting of cream and white flowers softens the boundaries of this patio, while the white garden furniture also helps to make the space appear larger than it really is.

Square plot

Here, the strong, circular ground plan helps to camouflage the squareness of the plot. Access to the pool and seat is via a brick path that reflects the circular theme, and matches the brick edging around the gravel area. The contrast between the brick path and surrounding gravel helps to disguise the fact that most of the garden is finished in hard surfacing. Any tendency towards this looking flat is avoided by the careful positioning of terracotta and stone containers filled with striking annuals, succulents and foliage plants.

Circular design
Used for beds, paving and furniture, circles form the theme of a square, walled garden.

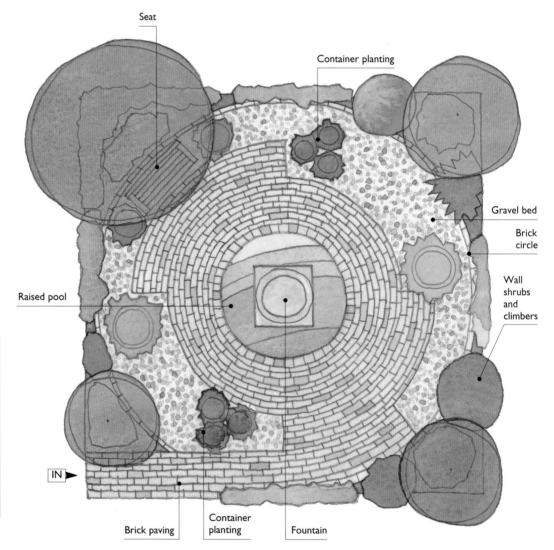

Seat

Container planting

Gravel bed

Brick circle

Wall shrubs and climbers

Raised pool

IN

Brick paving

Container planting

Fountain

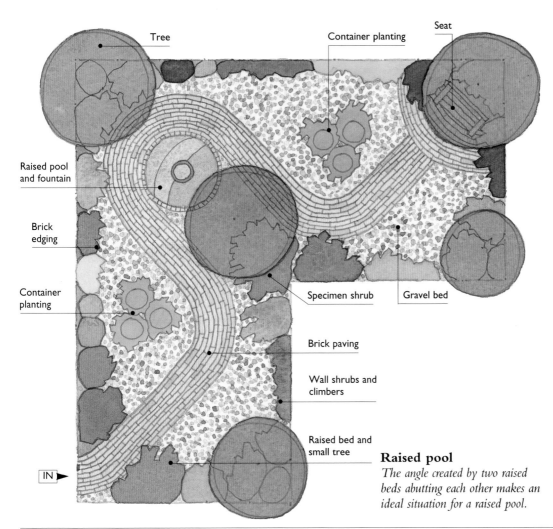

Tree

Container planting

Seat

Raised pool and fountain

Brick edging

Container planting

Specimen shrub

Gravel bed

Brick paving

Wall shrubs and climbers

Raised bed and small tree

IN ▶

L-shaped plot

In this awkwardly shaped garden, the circular theme is retained as far as possible, enhanced by the sweeping curves of the brick path and perimeter border.

The raised pool is now positioned so that it effectively links the two halves of the garden, and an additional raised bed planted with a small tree and ground cover shrubs acts as a focal point near the entrance.

Raised pool
The angle created by two raised beds abutting each other makes an ideal situation for a raised pool.

Rectangular plot

In this rectangular plot, the seating area is shifted to the far corner of the garden, the sweeping, curved path through the middle increasing the feeling of space.

The circular theme is retained in the shapes of the brick-paved seating area and the raised pool and fountain.

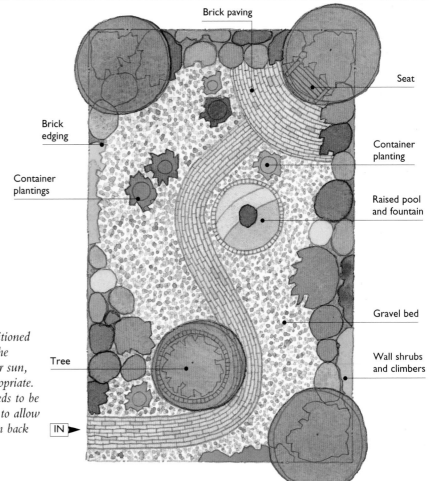

Brick paving

Seat

Container planting

Raised pool and fountain

Gravel bed

Wall shrubs and climbers

Brick edging

Container plantings

Tree

IN ▶

Seating areas
These can be positioned so that they get the benefit of shade or sun, whichever is appropriate. Enough space needs to be allocated to them to allow chairs to be drawn back from the table.

Low maintenance gardens

One way to reduce maintenance in a garden, especially in small gardens, is to use gravel or paving rather than grass. You should also avoid over-fussy designs with squiggly borders and individual trees or shrubs planted in lawns. Instead choose simple shapes with long, flowing curves. Rather than struggle to keep a lawn looking good, or having to constantly water plants in pots and containers, choose plants that will grow well in the conditions available, are reliable and long-lived, have a habit which requires little maintenance and cover the ground well.

Trouble-free wood and paving
This garden requires very little work other than sweeping, applying an annual coat of preservative to furniture and planting containers.

Long narrow plot

To keep it low-maintenance, much of this garden is devoted to the decking terrace, paths and water feature, and gravel is used as a mulch. The plot's narrowness is disguised by taking the decking almost full width across it. The change of direction of the stepping stone path between the pool and seating area, plus the tree half-way down the boundary wall break up the garden's tunnel-like effect.

Tree
Shrub border
Gravel bed
Stepping stones
Bark mulch in shrub border
Raised bed (shrubs and perennials)
Shrub border

Seat
Flag patio
Climbers on pergola posts
Raised bed (shrubs and perennials)
Water feature
Shrub border
Decking terrace

Rectangular plot

Here, the central space of the garden is covered in relatively maintenance-free gravel as opposed to being put down to lawn.

It is separated from the perimeter planting by a brick edge, which matches the coping of the two raised beds while keeping the gravel in place. Planting is of shrubs and perennials selected not only for their flower and foliage but also for their relative ease of maintenance and ground-covering abilities. A generous mulch of ornamental-grade bark over the surface of the planted area keeps in moisture and also helps to discourage weeds.

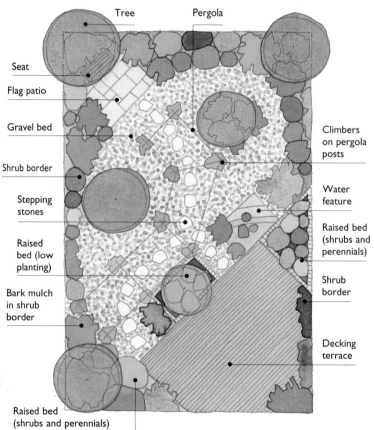

Seat
Flag patio
Gravel bed
Shrub border
Stepping stones
Raised bed (low planting)
Bark mulch in shrub border
Raised bed (shrubs and perennials)

Tree
Pergola
Climbers on pergola posts
Water feature
Raised bed (shrubs and perennials)
Shrub border
Decking terrace

Square plot

In this square variation, the design is simply 'clocked' 45°. By twisting the angle in this way, the garden appears less short and squat than it actually is. The pergola over the stepping stones will also deflect attention from the end boundaries.

Having the pool in the foreground provides a visual balance to the sitting area and ornamental tree in the opposite corner. The spaces for planting created by this arrangement are comparatively generous for such a small garden and help to disguise its squareness.

The design would suit plant enthusiasts without small children.

Oriental garden
A bamboo water spout and grasses on a bed of pebbles bring maintenance-free interest to a dull corner.

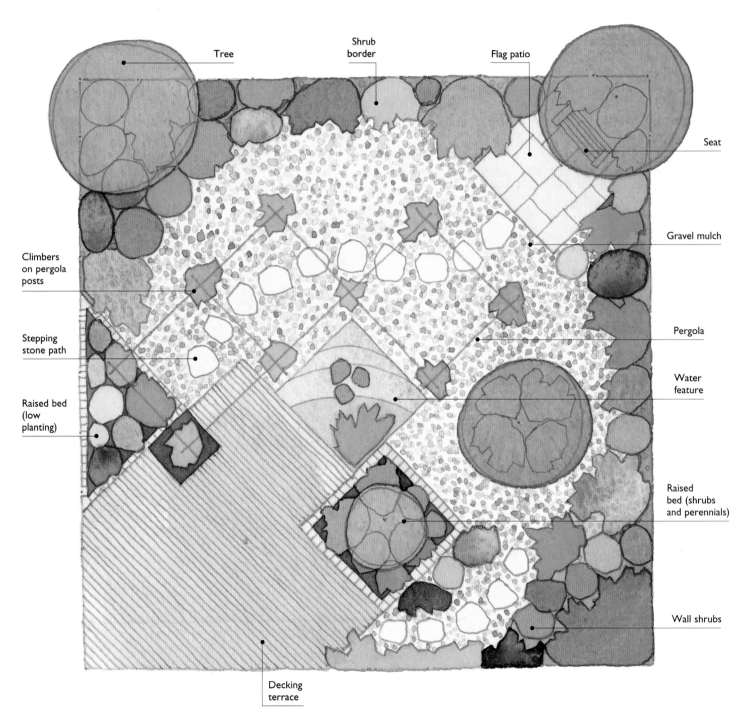

Tree

Shrub border

Flag patio

Seat

Gravel mulch

Climbers on pergola posts

Pergola

Stepping stone path

Water feature

Raised bed (low planting)

Raised bed (shrubs and perennials)

Wall shrubs

Decking terrace

Large gardens

Large gardens naturally provide more opportunities for a variety of garden features and ideas, both because of their size, and because they have fewer limitations or restrictions, such as shading from tall buildings, or being overlooked. There may be room to tuck away all the utility areas in their own separate space, leaving whole sections of the garden free for purely ornamental or recreational use. Similarly, a whole area could be devoted to fruit and vegetables without impinging on the rest of the garden. Within the ornamental garden you could opt for one theme throughout, or incorporate a variety of ideas. An effective way to do this is to gradually change style as you move from one end of the garden to the other.

Exuberant borders
A larger garden may need a lot of work but it does allow plenty of scope for massed plantings on a grand scale.

Wide, shallow plot

To effectively disguise the shape of this plot, the terrace and gravel garden are turned through an angle to focus the view diagonally into the two far corners of the garden.

Rather than being tucked away, as it might be in a smaller garden, the gazebo becomes a prominent feature, and the character of the garden changes from formal to natural across its width, rather than from end to end which is more usual. This means that the pond is situated in the corner beyond the gravel garden, but is still separated from the traditionally mown lawn by a wild-flower meadow area, as in the other designs here. The perimeter border is irregularly shaped, with room for generous planting of taller shrubs and perennials to further disguise the awkward shape of the boundaries.

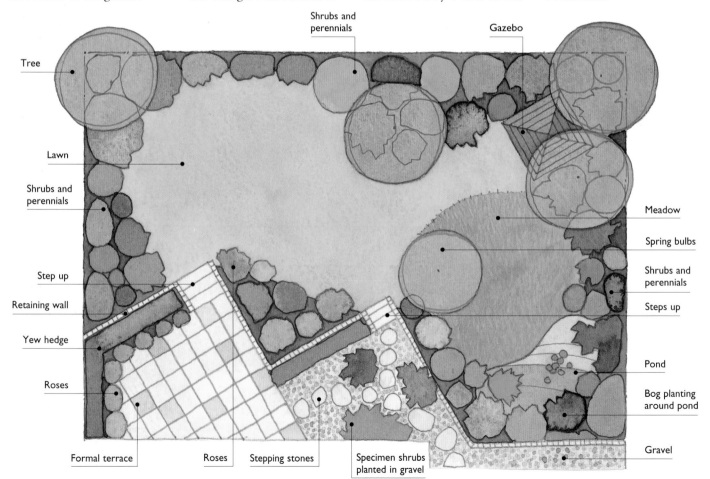

Tree

Shrubs and perennials

Gazebo

Lawn

Shrubs and perennials

Step up

Retaining wall

Yew hedge

Roses

Meadow

Spring bulbs

Shrubs and perennials

Steps up

Pond

Bog planting around pond

Gravel

Formal terrace

Roses

Stepping stones

Specimen shrubs planted in gravel

Long narrow plot

Here, the terrace runs across the full width of the garden, and the gravel area is brought into the foreground. This, the lawn and the wildflower meadow are all roughly circular and the junction of these is marked by trees and tall shrub planting which interrupts the view towards the far end of the garden and loosely divides the plot into smaller spaces. The glimpses of lawn visible from the area nearest the house entice exploration.

A mown path borders the longer grass of the wildflower meadow and carries the eye as well as the feet towards the gazebo in the far corner. The furthermost third of the garden has a wilder character. The natural-looking pond is brought away from the corner to form a focal point when viewed from the gazebo. Moisture-loving planting in the damp ground beside the pond makes it look part of the landscape.

Rectangular plot

The extra width allows the terrace and gravel garden to be side by side, both dropping down to the lawn by way of stone steps.

The generous expanse of lawn gives a luxurious, spacious feel, while its irregular margins blur the boundaries and carry the eye into the distance. On the left, a meadow area is left uncut until the wild flowers that make it colourful in early summer have set their seed. The character of the garden changes gradually from formal to almost natural with the pond and gazebo partially screened from the house by a small copse of trees underplanted with spring flowering bulbs. Water-loving gardeners with enough space might devote a larger area to the natural pond, or introduce a more formal water feature closer to the house.

Water-loving plants
A pond is the ideal habitat for plants such as Stratiotes, Menyanthes *and* Carex.

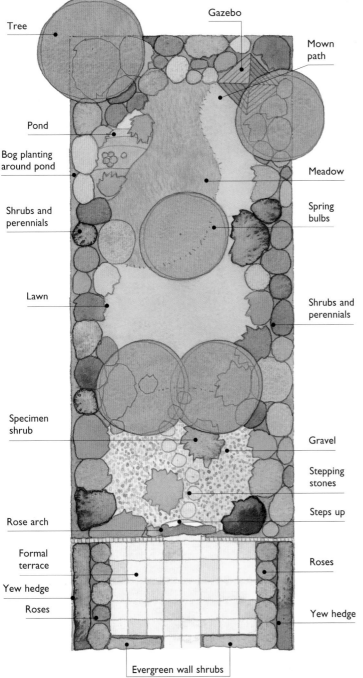

Tree
Gazebo
Mown path
Pond
Bog planting around pond
Meadow
Shrubs and perennials
Spring bulbs
Lawn
Shrubs and perennials
Specimen shrub
Gravel
Stepping stones
Steps up
Rose arch
Formal terrace
Roses
Yew hedge
Roses
Yew hedge
Evergreen wall shrubs

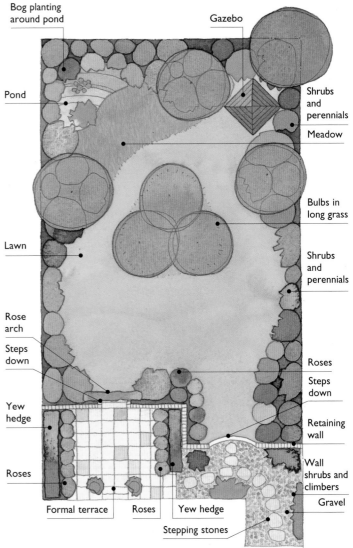

Bog planting around pond
Gazebo
Shrubs and perennials
Meadow
Pond
Bulbs in long grass
Shrubs and perennials
Lawn
Rose arch
Roses
Steps down
Steps down
Yew hedge
Retaining wall
Roses
Wall shrubs and climbers
Gravel
Formal terrace
Roses
Yew hedge
Stepping stones

Creating surface designs

Although in theory it is perfectly feasible to create a garden without any form of paving or hard surfacing, in reality it is needed in the vast majority of gardens to allow year-round, all-weather access, and to prevent wear and tear to soft elements such as lawns. Horizontal surfaces not only give access to other areas, but provide messages about how the garden is to be utilized. These should be comfortable to use, whether they are for a sitting area, for a path providing access around borders, or for steps up to a patio. The choice of surfacing will be determined partly by its function and how this relates to your overall garden design, and partly by the suitability of the material for its intended purpose.

Choosing the appropriate surface
Flat areas of curving lawn and gravel paths are relieved by islands of ground cover planting, while chipped bark, kept in place with timber edging, makes an excellent softer covering for the children's play area.

Ground cover planting

Although grass is an obvious choice for covering large areas, an alternative is a dense covering of low-growing plants. This will prevent or greatly reduce weed growth and act as an insulating layer to minimize wasteful evaporation of water from the soil's surface, keeping it cool in hot weather. Planting also absorbs the energy of heavy rainfall and in so doing protects the soil from erosion.

However, a lawn of closely mown grass will always have appeal, not least for its important visual role in both delineating and linking parts of the garden, but also for the delight we take in a cool green sward. A lawn is ideal for light recreational use and for more passive activities such as just sitting out. But concentrated or intense use can lead to wear and tear, particularly in wet conditions or when the grass is dormant in winter and unable to recover. Traditional lawns also require a fairly high degree of regular maintenance to keep them in shape and looking good, not forgetting that you may have to wait anything from a few weeks to several months before a newly seeded or turfed lawn can be used.

Timber decking

As an alternative to lawn or paving or gravel surfaces, timber planks and boards make excellent decking or walkways. They look and feel good, and blend in well with most other materials. If you use softwood, costs can compare quite favourably with good quality unit paving, though hardwood will usually be more expensive.

A fair degree of skill is required in both planning and constructing timber features and regular treatment against rot is necessary in all but the driest conditions. In damp, shady situations, wood surfaces may develop algal growths which, though not detrimental to the fabric of the construction, can become slippery and therefore potentially dangerous. So where possible, site your timber path or area in an open, dry, sunny position. Leave narrow joints between the boards to allow air to circulate and water to drain away quickly. If this is not possible you must be prepared to either scrub the surface clean on a regular basis or else treat it with a proprietary algicide to discourage algal growth.

Diagonal decking
Set in contrasting directions, these diagonal raised blocks provide a lively alternative surface material. Wood can be slippery when wet, but has a comforting, warm feel in mild, dry weather.

Gravel and bark chippings

These are not only cheaper and easier to put down than paving, but need little advance preparation. For small gardens, gravel is often more practicable than lawns. Obtainable in bulk or handy-sized bags, it can provide an instant paving solution, although it is best laid on a hardcore base, as it will gradually disappear into soft ground.

There are various types of gravel, but the one most suited to paths consists of small angular stones not larger than 25mm (1in) across. Shingle and larger cobbles are naturally worn rounded pebbles, uncomfortable to walk on but ideal for ornamental use. A surface of bark (or wood) chippings is a good protective mulch, pleasant to walk or play on and blending in well with landscape features. Fine bark can become soggy when wet, or blow away when dry. For paths, it is best laid over a hardcore base.

Paving

For rigid surfaces, paving units in the form of slabs, bricks, pavers, setts and tiles are hardwearing and long-lasting, and suitable for areas of constant use, all year round. The range of materials is extensive, and includes natural or reconstituted stone, and cement-based products often with a textured or 'weathered' finish.

The beauty of this type of surface is that it can be in use almost as soon as it is completed. Compared to grass or gravel, paving is more expensive and, for best results, more skill and effort is required in both preparation and laying.

Good paving should be reasonably smooth and be made from a non-slip material

Informal setting
Small paving slabs are excellent for informal settings as they can easily be laid to form curves or bends. The weatherbeaten grey stone blends well with the relaxed feel of this garden.

(so beware of using marble or slate). Even stone can become mossy and slippery in damp corners. Paving should be laid with a slight fall to throw off water. It needs a firm, prepared base to prevent long-term settlement or damage which could cause it to become unsafe.

Combining materials
Used imaginatively, most surface materials can be successfully teamed with others for practical or aesthetic purposes. For example, paving flags laid as stepping stones across a lawn will cut down on grass wear and tear, or they can be laid in similar style amidst gravel to make walking easier.

To keep costs down, use a few contrasting bricks, tiles or cobbles to liven up plain,

Stones, brick and timber
A variety of materials has been used at the meeting place of brick and timber-and-gravel paths. The shingle-filled circle echoing the round stone ewer catches water from a Japanese-style trickle fountain, and self-seeded ground covers have crept in amongst the gravel.

grey concrete slabs. Or use them as edging to retain an area of gravel. Where old timbers are plentiful, use them in conjunction with gravel or

bark chippings to form path surfaces, or as the front edges to steps, where a contrasting edging material is a useful safety feature.

Pavings and cobbles
Red bricks turn plain concrete paving into a lively but even path surface, while the different-sized cobbles provide a good link with the planting, their rounded forms echoing those of the ground level leaf shapes.

Hard surfaces

As a general rule, all paving materials, whether gravel, slabs, bricks or tarmacadam, will perform better and last longer if laid on a properly prepared base, rather than straight onto soil. Bare earth can be prone to movement, settlement and other problems caused by tree roots or a high water table. For gravel, paving, bricks, setts and concrete or stone flags, a layer of sand over a hardcore base is usually more than adequate for most garden situations. However, on exceptionally soft or disturbed ground, or where the paving you are using is very thin, such as quarry tiles or slate, a rigid concrete base may be necessary (see p.30). In either case, the object is to create a sufficiently solid base that will not settle or move to the detriment of the paving laid on it.

In laying most hard surfaces, you will need first to remove soil. How much and how deep is primarily determined by the depth of hardcore base required (which in turn depends on its purpose), plus the bed of sand or mortar on which the paving is to be laid, and the thickness of the paving itself.

Mixing materials
Reconstituted stone slabs, brick and timber decking are used to create an attractive terrace overlooking a pebble-lined water feature.

Preparing a hardcore base

All hard surfaces in the garden will usually require soil to be replaced by compacted hardcore. This can consist of crushed or broken bricks, pieces of concrete, stone or large flints, which is then laid in a bed about 4–6in (10–15cm) thick.

You will need a mix of less coarse hardcore and a finer material such as coarse sand, ash or brick dust to 'blind', that is, fill in, any voids between the large hardcore chunks, to leave a relatively smooth and level surface on which to

Datum peg
Used to indicate:
• *depth of the excavation*
• *level of the hardcore*
• *level of the finished paving*

lay your gravel or paving. Hardcore must be well-compacted to make it firm. Use a square hand tamp for small areas, but for large areas over 10sq m (30ft), such as a driveway, you will probably need to hire a plate vibrator (a much larger machine used for levelling, available from tool hire companies

Excavate the area for your path, patio or paved area by removing the topsoil to the required depth. This will be the depth of the hardcore, plus the thickness of the paving, setts or brick surface.

Place a datum peg (left) to indicate the different levels of excavated base, hardcore and paving, measuring from here with a spirit level. If the area is dug from soft soil, you will need to shutter it with timber boards (see p.30), sawn to the correct length. Hammer in

pegs for the shuttering around the edge of the area to a common level and then attach the wooden planks to them with nails. Backfill outside with spare soil (or hardcore) so that the boards will stay firm as the base is infilled. Begin adding the hardcore and compact (tamp) it as you go. Cover coarse hardcore with finer materials and tamp again until the surface is firm and level.

1 *The excavated and shuttered area is 15cm (6in) deep. The top of the datum peg is level with the surrounding soil.*

2 *Shovel in hardcore (this is quite fine) to a depth of 10cm (4in), as indicated by marks on the datum peg.*

3 *Use a hand tamp to compact small areas. Because this hardcore is fine it needs no infill, and is ready for the sand bed.*

Bricks

Both the colour and durability of bricks vary considerably and it is important that any bricks you buy match those of your house, or other features, such as a garden wall. For example, extra-tough engineering bricks in a blue-grey colour would not suit an informal cottage garden. Nowadays, the

Bricks for a sitting area
Small unit pavings such as bricks, setts and pavers are extremely useful where paths or patios are to be curved rather than rectangular.

choice of bricks for surface materials has been extended to include pavers, available in similar sizes as well as in squares or wedge

shapes for curved areas or edgings. Granite setts, small square stones, are similar to old-fashioned cobbles, and laid as for bricks.

Brick patterns

Rectangular bricks can be laid in many patterns, either flat (the wider face) or on edge (the narrower side). The patterns below all use whole bricks with half or diagonally cut bricks to complete the work at the ends or sides.

Stretcher bond
Strongly linear, this design will make a path seem wider.

Diagonal herringbone
More difficult to lay, this suggests rapid movement.

Horizontal herringbone
A lively pattern, popular in Tudor times.

Basket weave
A variation on stretcher bond, using whole bricks.

Laying bricks on a sand base

When laying paths and patios of brick or other units on a layer of sand over the hardcore base rather than mortaring them onto a concrete base, you will need some sort of edging to hold them in position. Here the same bricks are used. For greater stability this edging is

laid on a concrete footing. Calculate the path or patio area carefully so that the brick pattern you want can be achieved with as many whole bricks as possible. A simple pattern based on rightangles, such as basket weave, (see right) is an example. Here, provided that

the area is calculated as an exact multiple of brick lengths, no cutting will be needed. To make up some patterns, however, you will have to cut bricks in half, and designs with a diagonal bias call for triangular shapes to be cut. Having to do this makes the work more time-consuming and also requires extra skills and equipment.

1 *Edging bricks (here laid flat on) are placed along a string guide onto sand; the trowel is used to neaten the edge.*

2 *At the end of the path, lay another retaining edge of bricks at a precise right-angle to the first, to form a corner.*

3 *Use a notched screed board (cut at each end) to level the bed of sand before laying the infill bricks.*

4 *A half-brick completes the pattern. Split bricks with a hammer and bolster chisel, or a stone cutter or angle grinder.*

5 *Sprinkle sand over the bricks and brush in well until it fills the gaps.*

6 *Tamp the bricks down using a club hammer on a wooden block placed diagonally. Finally, brush in more sand.*

Concrete

For rigid surfaces, especially those expected to take heavy use, unit paving should be set onto a concrete base. The same applies to edgings, retaining walls, steps and any construction – such as a shed – needing the long-term stability of a base or footing.

As well as acting as a base, an area of concrete laid in place can look attractive as a surface material in its own right. Surface texture can be varied by a number of means – by tamping with a wooden plank to give a textured linear pattern (see opposite) or with a metal hand tamp to give a smooth finish. Use a brush for a surface that gives some grip. For an even but weathered look, wash and gently brush away some of the surface cement to expose the aggregate, before the concrete quite sets.

When laying areas of concrete it is vital to work in small sections, both for ease of working and for laying the cement mix smoothly. This allows for gaps between each section to cope with natural shrinkage and expansion. Called 'thermal movement joints', these can be worked into the overall design, either as straight lines (using wood shuttering) or in curves using plastic strips for shuttering. Like any other material, a concrete surface also needs its own concrete base to prevent movement and cracks.

Concrete surface
With a little planning, concrete laid in situ *can be made to look very attractive.*

Creating shuttering

Before the hardcore base and concrete can be laid in the excavated area, it is essential to place shuttering around it. Wet concrete needs strong timber shuttering (or formwork), because it is not only very heavy but will tend to spread sideways unless prevented from doing so.

Fix the shuttering to small stakes or pegs each about 1m (3ft) apart. The top edge of the formwork should reach the same height as the intended level of concrete.

The exact depth of the hardcore base and concrete layer will depend on the type of surface or structure the foundation will support. As a rough guide:
• **paths, patios or greenhouse:** 15cm (6in) of hardcore plus 10-15cm (4-6in) of concrete.
• **driveways, car port, etc:** 15cm (6in) of hardcore plus 15-20cm/6-8in concrete.

To gauge the depth of each layer correctly, use a datum peg, driven into the ground with its top at surrounding soil level (see p.29), marked with the depth of excavation, the depth of the hardcore bed, and of the concrete foundation and/or surface material.

One datum peg, placed centrally, will do for a small area, but for areas larger than 1sq m (3sq ft) place pegs at intervals of not more than 1m (3ft) apart.

1 *After digging out and tamping the bed, insert the datum peg and check that its top is level with the surrounding soil.*

2 *Use some of the excavated soil to fill the pit to just above the bottom mark on the peg, and tamp well with the feet.*

3 *Place pegs for attaching the shuttering around the edge and level them to the datum peg with hammer and spirit level.*

4 *Wooden planks (shuttering) are first sawn to the correct length and height before they are nailed to the pegs.*

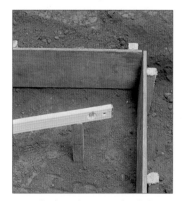

5 *Check with a spirit level that the shuttering is level all round, and then backfill outside the shuttering with soil to contain the weight of the hardcore and concrete.*

Laying a concrete base

Where the ground is soft, or under heavy use perhaps by vehicles, a concrete base should be laid on top of a minimum of 10cm (4in) thickness of compacted and blinded hardcore.

The area of concrete to be laid at any one time must be easily manageable – for an experienced person an absolute maximum would be 4.5m (15ft) in any direction. Apart from the difficulty of handling larger areas, a continuous surface will crack more easily.

After tamping to release air bubbles, wet concrete needs to be roughened with a plank as shown in order to key well with the mortar holding the final surface material in place.

Once the bed has been infilled with hardcore and concrete, the shuttering can be removed.

1 *Fill the shuttered area with loose hardcore and firm down well, using a square tamp as shown, or a plate vibrator.*

2 *Remove the datum peg and infill the hole. Note the markings on the peg indicating the different levels of the layers.*

3 *After mixing the cement mixture on a suitable surface or board, shovel it in, and level it with the shovel as you go.*

4 *Use a wooden plank to 'saw off' and smooth the surface of the cement, moving it from left to right and then dragging it back towards you.*

5 *Move a short-handled wooden tamp up and down (or left to right) in a regular chopping motion to bring air and surplus water to the top.*

6 *Repeat the sawing and smoothing of the concrete's surface, finally leaving a linear pattern to help the surface material adhere to the concrete.*

Concrete mixes

Different surfaces and foundations need different ratios of ingredients. A mix of 1:6 cement: sand/gravel (1 part cement to 6 parts ballast) is 'leaner' than one of 1:4.

Measure the quantities by volume (eg in a bucket). Add water until the mortar is just firm enough to hold its shape. If you need to spread the cement mix fast to level it, use a sloppier mix that almost flows.

• **concrete base/foundation** 1:2:4 cement: sand: gravel. If you are using all–in ballast (where sand and gravel are premixed), use 1:6 cement: ballast.
• **mortar pads under slabs** 1:4 or 1:5 cement: builders' sand (on hardcore or cement base)
• **stepping stones** 1:6 cement: sharp sand (a pad under each stone; no hardcore base)
• **concrete footing for steps or a brick retaining edge** 1:6 cement: sharp sand (onto hardcore base)
• **pointing for paving slabs** 1:3 or 1:4 cement: builders' sand.

Lean mortar mix
This is the correct consistency for mortaring paving slabs onto a hardcore or concrete base.

Cement for pointing

Finishing off areas of paving with mortar neatens their appearance and prevents weeds growing between the cracks. An alternative to using wet mortar is to brush a mix of dry cement and sand into the cracks between pavings and then water it in.

If you use sand instead of mortar, you will be able to grow creeping plants between the stones. Small tough perennials, such as creeping thyme (*Thymus* spp.) and Baby's Tears (*Soleirolia soleirolii*) are ideal.

In this case, you should make the joints slightly further apart than normal – a couple of centimetres (around an inch) is normal. It will, however, mean that weeds will also germinate in the cracks!

Pointing paving slabs
A stiff mortar mix of 1:3 or 1:4 cement: sand avoids staining.

Neatening off
Use a smaller trowel to neaten the mortar between the slabs.

Paving

Apart from practicality, any paving materials you select for your garden should reflect the theme of its design in style and colour. They should complement the fabric of the house, and be a low-key background to your planting. And, of course, they must be cost-effective.

Pavings should be made from a strong, durable and preferably non-slip material. Popular and not too costly are pre-cast concrete slabs in a range of sizes, colours and textures. Paved paths and patios must be laid on a firm, prepared foundation of hardcore or even concrete.

Near the house, especially, paving should have a slight fall to allow water to drain off into planting, a lawn or a drainage channel. For smooth surfaces such as concrete slabs, a fall of about 1 in 100 is adequate, but for rougher pavings, such as natural riven stone, it might need to be 1 in 80 or even 1 in 60.

If there is a manhole or drain within the area to be paved, make sure this is not covered over. So that the look of the area is not spoiled, most pavings can be fitted into a special metal frame to disguise the drain or cover.

An invitation to relax
Flat areas of concrete paving slabs are interspersed with large cobble stones, gravel and low planting, to give texture, variety and a relaxed, harmonious feel to this small patio.

Laying paving

Accurately setting out the shape and level of your patio using shuttering and string guides will make laying the flags or pavings much easier. (If you have not used shuttering for the hardcore base, you can use taut string between the edging pegs to indicate the area to be paved.)

Start off with the row nearest to the house and work from there. The flagstones are lowered onto dabs of soft mortar (for the correct mix, see p.31) on top of the hardcore base.

Make sure that at this stage they are slightly higher than the finished level – they can then be tapped down until they line up with the guide strings and pegs. Once the mortar has set ('gone off'), the flags will remain at that level.

For a completely waterproof finish, leave a 13mm (1/2 in) gap between flags, and point by filling the gap with a stiff mix of strong mortar when laying is completed (see p.45).

1 *Position a trial paving on the hardcore bed to indicate the placing of the string. Remove.*

2 *Put down dabs of mortar for the corners and centre. Reposition the first slab along the string.*

3 *All the while checking levels, knock the slab down to the correct height with the hammer.*

4 *Complete the row and then reposition the string for the second row. When you have placed two pavings in the second row, check the level diagonally across four slabs.*

The completed patio
The cracks between the pavings can be left or pointed with wet or dry mortar to prevent weeds from growing.

Steps

Gardens are rarely level and when laying paths, for example, you will need to take account of this – especially on sloping sites. A slope of 1 in 12 is about the maximum gradient that is comfortable to walk on. Anything steeper than this will require steps.

These might be in flights of two or more at a single point, or they could be well-spaced so that you climb one, walk two or three paces and then climb a second flight, and so on. Steps can be purely functional – just terraced ground edged with timber risers – or they can be a formal feature in their own right, perhaps enhanced with planted pots. The important thing is that they should fit in with their surroundings in both scale and materials, and be wide enough for the user to feel relaxed. Steps that are too narrow will have the opposite effect.

The height of a step, its 'riser', must feel safe and comfortable and, as a general rule, should be not less than 7.5cm (3in), or more than 17.5cm (7in) – not as high as stairs indoors. For similar reasons, the depth, or 'tread', should ideally be not less than 30cm (1ft).

Informal planting to enhance brick and stone
Steps can add to the charm of a small garden, especially when the same materials are used for connecting paths. The informal planting complements the harmonious feel.

Making paving slab steps

As well as allowing easier access, adding a flight of steps to a bank makes a strong design element. Plain concrete flags can be softened with low planting.

Work out the height of the bank (see p.17) and divide into the number of steps required. The shorter the riser, the deeper the tread needs to be. Insert canes to mark the position of each step. Excavate all the treads, roughly – but not so much that the bank collapses!

The first tread is supported on bricks and hardcore set on a concrete footing. Dig out a 5cm (2in) trench beneath the front and sides of the first flag position, allowing for a 2.5cm (1in) overlap of the flag's front edge.

Use a concrete mix of 1:5 or 1:6 cement: sharp sand for the footing, adding water until it is quite stiff. Leave overnight to set.

Lay prepared mortar on the footing. Make a fishbone pattern with the trowel so that the mortar can spread easily. On top of this lay four bricks, two at the front, one on each side, mortaring the joints as you go. (If you need to use more than four bricks, mortar them individually). Tamp the bricks into place with the trowel handle, and check with a spirit level.

Infill the space with hardcore and firm, using a piece of timber and a club-hammer handle. Lay a 2.5cm (1in) thick mortar bed along the top of the bricks and at the back edge of the hardcore. Add a mortar pad in the centre. Lower the flagstone into position, allowing a 2.5cm (1in) overhang at the front. Tamp with the hammer handle and check levels. Neaten the sides and mortar with a pointing trowel, sloping the pointing so that water will run off. Fill any space behind the tread with hardcore. Continue the process until all the steps are complete.

1 *Mortar the first brick risers in position on the footing, two at the front and one at each side.*

2 *The mortar and hardcore bed, ready for the first flag, to overhang by 2.5cm (1in) in front.*

3 *Put mortar along the back of the first tread to secure the two bricks as risers for the second tread. Infill again with hardcore.*

4 *Firm the hardcore, mortar the sides and bricks with a dab in the centre. Allow 2.5cm (1in) overhang for the second flag.*

5 *As a final touch, a flag tread has been placed at the bottom of the steps on a mortar bed and mortared against the footing.*

Gravel

A useful and economical substitute for paving is gravel, available in a choice of colours, textures and sizes, from almost round, river-worn pebbles to small, angular chips of mechanically crushed granite or sandstone.

There are three points to consider when using gravel. First, loose gravel tends to disperse and needs a slightly raised edge to retain it. Second, if gravel is laid too deep it can be difficult to walk on – particularly if it is smooth and round. Finally, constant foot or car traffic may push gravel into the base below, so you will have to top it up. How much and often will depend on whether the base is soft topsoil or firm, blinded hardcore. One way of taking these factors into account is to combine the gravel with concrete, stone flags or bricks laid like stepping stones, so that you actually walk on them rather than on the gravel itself. If you wish, you can plant into gravel to create a garden that is maintenance-free, as the gravel will suppress weeds.

Plants in gravel
An area of gravel will attract plants that enjoy the mulch-like quality of the dry stones.

Laying gravel

You will need to decide how you want to retain the gravel – with tiles, bricks or wood. Here, the shuttering round the path or gravel area stays to serve as edging. For a brick retaining edge, see p.29. Begin by excavating a trench or bed for the base, 7.5cm (3in) deep, and see p. 30 for setting up the formwork. With a shovel and and tamp, spread, level and compact a hardcore layer to within 2.5cm (1in) of the formwork top. This gap will leave room for quite enough gravel – there is no need to be extravagant with it. Check the level and lay the gravel with the shovel. Finish by tamping gently.

1 *Tamp the surface down well and check that it is even with a spirit level.*

2 *Use a sand layer for blinding if the hardcore is fairly coarse as this will hold the gravel better.*

Laying stepping stones

Begin by digging out the area, and tamping the earth base. Fix string guides for the paving levels (see p.32).

Mix up a stiff mortar in the ratio 1:6 cement: ballast for the footing pad. Gauge its depth by the thickness of the paving. Use the string guide to set the slabs at the correct height, but set them higher at first, so that they can be gently tamped down. Infill round the slabs with fairly fine hardcore such as crushed brick, and tamp so that the level is about 2.5cm (1in) below the top of the slabs. Then spread the gravel layer.

Bredon gravel, used here, is 'self-binding'. It has a layer of clay particles around the granite chips which eventually washes off in the rain to reveal its true, dark colour.

1 *Lay each slab on a pad of stiff mortar, directly onto the earth – no need for hardcore.*

3 *Infill around the slab with hardcore and sand, then tamp to just below the slab top.*

2 *Taut string guides indicate the alignment, height and level of the slab.*

4 *Add the gravel layer and smooth it, so it is flush with the top of the slab.*

Neat path with plantings
Stepping stones sit within the now-weathered gravel. The whole can then be framed by border plantings to rich effect.

Decking

With some forethought and a little long-term care, wood can make a very worthwhile alternative to traditional paving materials. It is one of the most versatile of natural materials, and timber features will enhance any garden.

Softwoods, predominantly from coniferous forest trees, are readily available in temperate climates. Less durable than hardwoods, they generally need some form of treatment with paints or stains. Hardwoods, coming from broad-leaved trees from other parts of the world, are more expensive; always check that

the wood comes from a sustainable forest planting. They can frequently be used without additional treatment, though stains or natural oils may be necessary to maintain an attractive appearance.

However, all wood is vulnerable to rot when in contact with damp soil so, in any construction, it will pay you to treat even hardwood against this, and ensure there is plenty of air space under and around the decking.

Warmth of wood surfaces
Timber decking has a warm feel in sunny weather and teams well with the jungle-like planting, terracotta pots and pebbles.

Laying a raised timber deck

When designing layouts for small or awkward spaces, decking offers a great deal more flexibility than, for example, stone flags or pavings which have fixed dimensions. Decking can be laid at ground level or as a raised platform, as a straight rectangle for a simple path, or staggered in an intricate pattern over a large area.

The joists should be heavy treated timber, and the planks should be pressure treated. Sawn timber will provide a more textured surface than planed, though you might need to give sawn softwood a precautionary rub over with coarse glasspaper to remove any serious splinters.

To help protect the joists from rot it is a good idea to raise them above soil level by laying them across a base of bricks on concrete pads. If you want to deck a large area, the construction is best done in stages.

For decking at ground level, the depth of the excavation needs to equal the height of all the materials. This will be the height of the concrete pad and brick (or concrete block), the joist, the rafter and the plank surface.

1 *The holes for the concrete pads should be about 45 x 45cm (17 x 17in) and 15cm (6in) deep, with their centres 1m (3ft) apart. Dig out, tamp soil and place shuttering for each one (see p.30). Check heights are uniform with string and a spirit level, and lay the cement mix.*

2 *Decide which way you want the planks to run – they will follow the joists (with the rafters at right angles in between). Set up two string guides, 10cm (4in) apart, in the same direction as the planks, along the centre of the pads, and lay the bricks within them.*

3 *The joists can now be laid along the bricks. The timber should overlap the pads and bricks at each end by at least 30cm (1ft), to conceal them.*

4 *Lay rafters 15cm (6in) in from the joist ends. The gap between the rafters should not be more than half the length of the planks they will support. Fix the rafters to the joists using galvanized nails (screws for heavy use) inserted at an angle.*

5 *Set a string down the middle of each rafter as a guide for nailing the planks. Use galvanized nails that are twice as long as the planks are thick. Note that the planks are the same length as the joists.*

6 *To conceal the joists of raised decking you can attach boards to the ends and sides. A soffit board 1.5cm (½in) thick is used here. Nail the board to the joist ends so that it lies flush with the edges of the planks.*

Soft ground cover

The term ground cover can be applied to any method of covering bare soil in a garden whether using living plants or inanimate natural or artificial materials, or indeed a combination of both. Ground covers, from coloured stone chippings to prostrate roses, are the very essence of low-maintenance gardening – unless of course you include lawns, which are for the most part particularly labour-intensive. A mulch is generally a form of ground cover that utilizes inanimate materials to do the job, regardless of whether they are natural, such as gravel, bark chippings or grass clippings, or artificial, like polythene.

The right choice of ground cover can add much to the overall appearance of a garden, especially in covering awkward places such as dry shade under trees or steep banks, and also in hiding unattractive features such as concrete path edges or manhole covers.

Ground-hugging plants and bark mulch
Plants that cover ground and need little attention are a bonus. Here, mounds of santolina (S. rosmarinifolia) *and purple French lavender* (Lavandula stoechas) *harmonize with stones and bark chippings.*

Designing with ground cover

For plants to be successful as ground cover, their foliage needs to be attractive and to provide cover over a long season. Their habit needs to be either clump-forming, prostrate, creeping or trailing – but their spread should not be so rapid that they them-selves become invasive weeds. Beware, too, of plants that are excessive self-seeders.

Ivies for shady places
Variegated ivy is a good choice beneath a thick evergreen hedge of Lonicera *'Baggesen's Gold'.*

Some creeping variegated plants, including vincas, ivies (*Hedera*) and bugle (*Ajuga*) fit this category, but many plants with colourful flowers that are not so ground-hugging also serve the purpose, among them geraniums, lamiums, low-growing cotoneaster and ceanothus, prostrate junipers such as *Juniperus horizontalis* and *J. procumbens*, heucheras, alchemilla, heathers and *Stachys byzantina*. Some species of flowering ornamental grasses, too, spread quickly into clumps, such as miscanthus, stipa and *Carex stricta* 'Aurea'. Even bulbs, such as cyclamens, snowdrops and bluebells can be left to spread under deciduous trees.

Ground cover plants form a permanent planting so you should prepare soil with care, eliminating all perennial weeds (contrary to popular belief, ground cover planting will not in itself get rid of an existing perennial weed problem). Until all the bare soil is covered by planting, the bed should be kept weed-free by hoeing or by mulching with a 25-50mm thick layer of organic matter.

A cover of flowers under trees
Spring flowers like white Spanish bluebells (Hyacinthoides hispanica) *are excellent under trees. By the time the tree canopy casts heavy shade, the flowers and foliage will have died down.*

Grassed surfaces

It is tempting to think of lawns merely in terms of the demands they make – as grass that needs cutting on a regular basis during spring and summer, or from which the autumn leaves must be cleared. But a well-thought-out and cared-for lawn is an asset and cán mean the difference between an acceptable garden and a brilliant one.

A cool, soft green sward is the perfect place for relaxation on a hot day, as well as the best companion to bright flower and foliage colours. The initial outlay is far less than for most hard surfaces, and the amount of time you devote to it depends on where you live and how much of a perfectionist you are. It is important to choose grass that is appropriate to the amount of wear and tear it is likely to experience, and always take mowing requirements into account. You also need to ensure the lawn is sensibly sited: grass needs some sunshine and should be laid on level ground.

A successful lawn need not be a perfectly uniform, outdoor carpet with parallel, mowed lines. Some gardeners are perfectly happy to allow in flowers, or even 'weeds'. Clover, which is a satisfying deep green colour, will actually improve the nutrient value of a lawn! And either simple daisies or more deliberate plantings, like spring bulbs or wild flowers, will embellish a lawn.

Lawns can define space
In this formal garden the mown lines lead the eye to a focal point beyond the steps and a second lawn, increasing the sense of distance.

Flowering lawns

Creating a wild flower meadow in a part of the garden where wear and tear are light is many people's idea of a country haven. Wildflower seeds are available in various mixtures to suit different soil types and drainage. Sow seed onto prepared ground (not lawn) but don't add compost or fertilizer – the majority of desirable wild flowers need low-nutrient soils to thrive.

Mix the wildflower seed with a large volume of grass seed selected from slow-growing, fine-leaved varieties. This will provide the basic sward through which the wild flowers will grow, and help prevent coarser grasses and weed seeds from germinating. Alternatively, plant very small plants or bulbs into an existing lawn. (A bulb planter will make this easier.)

Such lawns work best when the flowers share similar flowering times, because they should not be cut until after flowering, when seeds for next year's plants will have formed, or for bulbs, when the leaves that restore the plant's energy have died down. A mown path either through or around the meadow helps provide definition as well as access and makes the area look deliberately part of a designed garden rather than simply a neglected area.

Tall daisies and flowering grasses
A clipped grass path through a sunny meadow planting of long grasses and oxeye daisies meanders into a hidden area – perhaps to a surprise, cool woodland glade.

A flowery meadow
Spring anemones, wild tulips (T. tarda) and emerging orchids have turned this stretch of lawn into a carpet of flowers. The spring flowering means that the grass can be cut by midsummer, before it becomes too long.

Lawns

As when choosing a carpet or other floor covering, creating a lawn involves consideration of wear and tear and cost as well as appearance.

Grass seed may be sown in autumn or spring. An autumn sowing will mean the lawn will be ready for use the following summer, whereas a spring-sown lawn cannot be used until the end of summer. Laying turf is quicker but more expensive. Different grass seed mixes are available; some produce a resilient turf, ideal for heavy wear or children's play areas, while others give a finer lawn which looks more manicured but is less hardwearing. A fine lawn also requires more care – during the summer it will need to be mown every two or three days whereas ordinary turf only has to be cut about once a week.

Wildflower meadow
Studded with wild flowers, grass cut only once or twice a year forms a natural meadow.

Sowing a lawn

The key to success lies in the preparation of the ground prior to seeding or turfing. Prepare the soil by thorough cultivation to at least 25cm (10in). Improve poor soils with compost or organic matter and heavy, clay soils with sharp sand or grit. Add suitable fertilizer and rake it in.

All perennial weeds should be eradicated as they will persist even when the ground is turfed over, while annual weeds will quickly infest newly seeded areas of grass unless the ground is cleaned before sowing. Rake and roll the proposed lawn area or alternatively firm using your heels, to achieve a smooth, firm, level bed, removing any stones and other debris. Seed is best sown in the spring or early autumn when soil temperatures and moisture are at their best for germination. Scatter the seed thinly over the ground before lightly raking it into the top 5mm ($\frac{1}{4}$in) of soil. Germination is often aided by rolling the ground again just after sowing.

1 *Once the soil has been thoroughly cultivated, cleared and improved, rake it to a fine tilth, levelling as you go and removing all except the smallest stones.*

2 *Marked out metre (3ft) squares help you apply the right amounts of fertilizer to provide short and long-term nutrition for new grass. Rake in.*

3 *Sow half the appropriate seed quantity evenly within each metre square. Then sow the remainder at right angles to the first sowing and rake in.*

Laying turf

Turf can be laid at any time of year, if it is available, but avoid the depths of winter when the ground is frozen or waterlogged, and hot summer months unless you can water every day for up to three or four weeks. The turves must be kept moist until they have rooted, or they will shrink.

Take care never to disturb your prepared ground, and always stand on a plank. First lay a row of turves around the lawn perimeter (if rectangular), or along a straight edge. Fill in the area in rows with staggered joints, much like a brick wall. Settle the turf into position by tamping

Placing a roll of turf
Once the perimeter is laid, infill the area in a staggered pattern of closely butted turf rolls. Kneel on a board placed on previously laid turf.

it gently with the back of a rake head or a broom. Finish off by lightly brushing in sieved topsoil, filling in any gaps along the joins. Then water in well.

Shaping irregular lawns
Shape the turf around an informal flowerbed using a length of hosepipe as a template for cutting curves. Stand on a board and cut with a half-moon cutter (as here), a sharpened lawn-edger, or an old carving knife.

Edgings

As ground level boundaries, edgings play an important role in the garden layout. Whether of hard materials or planted, they help define and give emphasis to a lawn, path or border and often enhance a dull driveway. An edging is essential where loose materials meet, such as where gravel adjoins a flower bed. Without some form of definition, the gravel and soil will quickly become mixed and unattractive. The solution is to provide a rigid edge to separate them.

Provided that it is durable or can be maintained, virtually any material can be used as edging. Bricks, setts, concrete pavers and cobbles can all be used loose or set into mortar and concrete for a stronger, more permanent edge. Bricks can be placed horizontally along their long or short edges, set at different heights for a crenellated look, or positioned at an angle to give a zigzag effect. Large pieces of slate or paving flags buried on edge to half their depth are particularly useful for creating a retaining wall for a mini raised bed or to prevent soil washing down a bank.

For planted edgings, ground spreading plants such as bugle (ajuga), violas and hostas are all suitable, as well as taller flowering plants such as lavender and a variety of other aromatic shrubs or herbs – parsley, rosemary, sage and thyme – can also make good edging plants. Allowing these plants to flop over onto the pathway softens the divide between a hard and soft edging for a pleasing informal effect.

Soft and hard edgings
A twisting 'plait' of cobbles contains but also complements an informal planting of carmine pinks by a path of granite setts.

Formal planted edgings
Clipped dwarf box hedges are a traditional edging for vegetable gardens and flower beds. They are especially useful where controlled flowing lines are called for, such as in knot gardens.

Lawn edgings

Lawns should have a neat, defined edge; this can be achieved with a special tool called a half-moon blade which slices through the long grass vertically.

Where a lawn butts up against a wall, fence or terrace path, it is almost always impossible to mow right up to the edge, without leaving an unsightly strip of long grass or needing to cut with hand shears. By laying a level edge of bricks or paving stones, about 10mm ($\frac{1}{2}$ in) below the height of the lawn, you will be able to cut right to the edge of the grass and not damage the blades of your mower. This principle of a mowing edge can be used wherever lawn edges prove difficult to trim because of adjacent obstructions. Defining the edges of a lawn in this way also helps to give the garden a neat appearance and helps to make a clear distinction between grass and borders. Curved lawn edgings can be formed from thin, treated timber planks or plastic strips, which are unobtrusive and easy to lay. As an alternative to hard edgings, the boundary of a lawn could be defined with a border of shrubby plants, such as *santolina,* which stand clear of the grass, leaving space for the mower to cut up to the edges.

A mowing edge
A neat brick edge protects silvery Stachys byzantina *from the mower's blades.*

Tall lavender for a low hedge
A continuous planting of shrubby lavender forms the boundary between a lawn and a dense flower border that includes fruit trees.

Creating vertical structures

Apart from giving height to a garden, vertical structures give width or depth, divide the garden, screen and provide seclusion, and act as focal points and backdrops. They can be used to frame or accentuate other structures or parts of the garden as well as views beyond the garden boundaries.

The size or height of a structure does not need to be great to create an effect in a garden setting – even a simple change of level of only one or two steps can make an otherwise flat garden seem more interesting. Nor does it have to be solid to achieve its intentions, and in some instances this can be a distinct disadvantage. If, for example, you screen an oil tank with a fence panel, you may actually draw attention to it, whereas it might be more effective to break up the outline with a trellis panel, or a group of shrubs.

Depending on where you live, the pattern of sunlight in your garden during the day will vary according to the time of year, and you should try and take this into account when planning your structures – you probably won't want to place a summerhouse in a position that casts a large shadow over your patio for much of the day. Also, do not forget that trees are generally long-lived and will continue to increase in size, so what may have started out as a neat dome could grow to dominate a whole garden in years to come.

Shelter and shade

The introduction of vertical structures will not only have an effect on the appearance of the garden, but also on the amount of light, and sometimes moisture, reaching different parts of the garden.

In some cases, such as the position of a boundary fence or the aspect of your garden, these areas of shade or shadow will be pre-determined and you will have no control over them. However, there are instances where you can choose the location of your structure deliberately to create a sunny or shady place, and also manipulate space in such a way as to form an area for plants or for sitting out that is sheltered from prevailing winds or draughts. Creating draught-free spaces is particularly useful in mild climates where you want to take advantage of any winter sunshine. Conversely, on a hot summer's day, and especially in small town gardens, introducing one or two trees not only provides precious shade but encourages welcome light breezes. Use canes and thick strings to define the heights and gauge the shapes of your intended structures, firstly to see how they will appear to the eye and secondly to try and ascertain their effect on sunlight entering the garden so that you can make adjustments that may avoid future problems.

The higher the structure, the smaller the space it encloses will appear. Larger built structures, such as summerhouses, gazebos and conservatories, may require planning permission, so it is a good idea to seek advice first.

Hedges as windbreaks
A thick hedge is excellent for creating shelter for plants as it filters the wind. A more solid structure, such as a fence or wall, tends to deflect wind, causing strong downward airflow.

Verticals of varying heights
As well as providing screening, open timberwork above the fence supports climbing plants. The continuous low retaining wall acts as both raised flowerbed and sheltered seat.

Linking vertical elements

Repeating a colour, material or style in your vertical structures is a good way of developing a common theme in a garden and this approach can be extended to include horizontal surfaces such as paths and paving, resulting in a much more unified effect than would be the case with a random approach.

At the same time, creating a surprise as you turn a corner, with careful placing of a garden seat or statue, adds interest without detracting from the overall design. A simple way of achieving a sense of order and pattern is to repeat plantings, or terracotta or other decorative containers, so that they stand out from the background as strategic focal points, not necessarily all visible at the same time.

Evergreen and foliage plants are particularly useful in creating links, whether in a continuous planting, such as a hedge or screen, or individual plantings, particularly of specimens with strong architectural shapes or large leaves.

Using planting to unify
Tall foliage plants are used to partly screen and soften the outline of a greenhouse. The restrained flower colours, mainly acid greens and yellows, further unify the scene.

Planted structures

A host of plants can be trained to grow up and over garden structures, whether fences and trelliswork, walls, old tree stumps, living trees or hedges, and of course arches, pergolas and arbours made for the purpose.

Plants will both furnish and soften, or even disguise – which is an effect you can put to good use with other large garden structures such as a new summerhouse or garden shed, whose impact will be lessened if climbing plants are allowed to clamber over them.

Planting with a theme
A bold planting of architectural shrubs with contrasting foliage complements the oriental look of this grey-green wooden gazebo.

Space-creating devices
Various tactics can be used in gardens to give an illusion of more depth and space. One way is by using plant colour. Misty blues and silvery greens at the end of a vista suggest distance, especially in contrast with a foreground planting of sharp reds, oranges and yellows.

Other devices use perspective to exaggerate space and depth. For example, when a path gradually narrows in width as it recedes away from the house or point of view, it will appear longer than it is. Small openings that give views through otherwise solid fences or doors, and trellis wall 'arches' or painted murals are other tricks that can be used to open out space and give a less hemmed in feel, especially to small gardens. In a courtyard or patio garden, a cleverly placed wall mirror will reflect any planting – perhaps also the surface of a small pool – again giving a feeling of more space.

Peephole in a fence
The small window gives a view through this otherwise solid fence.

Trellis wall niche
The slats are placed to form an 'arch', partly hidden by clematis.

Boundaries

Garden boundaries, as with any other land boundaries, are a means of defining the extent of a particular parcel of land, and in most instances they have a legal significance.

Assuming that you know where they are, how you treat the boundaries of your own garden will depend partly on cost but also on your personal preferences. If you are a private person you might wish to conceal your garden with a high, solid wall or fence above eye level. On the other hand, a low, knee-high hedge might be all that you need. Security and safety must influence your selection, particularly if you have small children or dogs. You might need to strengthen a hedge with a wire mesh fence, or make sure that a fence or wall is built in such a way that it cannot be climbed easily. As well as practical aspects of garden boundaries, you should remember that they are an integral part of any garden design. You may therefore need to decide whether your boundaries are to become decorative garden features in their own right, or treated in a very low-key manner so that they are tucked away in the background. The general ambience or atmosphere of a garden can also be affected by the size and nature of any boundary enclosure. Think of the different effect you would create with a dense 3m (10ft) high conifer hedge and a 1m (3ft) high slender picket fence, in two otherwise identical gardens.

Fencing

Instant privacy is certainly one major reason why fences are popular and are often preferred to hedges, which can take several years to achieve the same effect. They are invariably cheaper to erect than walls of similar height, particularly if built from soft wood as opposed to hard wood. They do not require the same skill to construct, but may need periodic treatment with preservative to prevent rot.

As a way of demarcating two or more areas, there is nothing simpler than a fence of plain wooden posts with a couple of wires strung between them. But in most gardens, fences can serve more than one purpose and therefore their design and construction can become increasingly complex or ornate, depending on budget.

Rustic fencing
A criss-cross fence of rounded timber staves provides an informal boundary that allows plants behind to peep through.

Hedges

For most gardeners, hedges conveniently divide into formal and informal types, each of which may then be subdivided according to whether they are evergreen or deciduous. Though perhaps not requiring much money to maintain, hedges still need to be trimmed, therefore requiring a commitment of time.

Informal hedge
The flowing shape of this flowering hedge, aided by the conifer, obscures the solid outline of the next-door property to give a cheerful, relaxed boundary.

Walls

A brick, stone or concrete block wall will initially cost more than other barriers but if well built, should last more or less indefinitely and need little maintenance during its extensive lifetime.

Such a wall is relatively expensive, though, and the level of skill required to build even the simplest may be beyond the reach of the vast majority of gardeners.

However, on sloping sites a fairly easily built, low, retaining wall will hold back soil while creating terracing and changes of level.

A not-so-solid wall
A brick wall need not be entirely solid. Here an arched window, framed by climbing roses, gives a view of the lawn beyond.

Exits and entrances

Entrances to gardens are frequently treated almost as an afterthought in a design, nothing more than a way in or out. However there is lots of potential to make them something more than just a simple gap in a fence, wall or hedge. First, of course, you must consider any practical aspects, as you would for a boundary, which in most instances is what an entrance forms part of. So whether it is an open archway for example, or a gate in a wall, will depend on how secure you wish the garden to be.

From the outside, entrances can be used to give clues as to the garden within, either by the way they are used, perhaps framing a view of a small part of the garden beyond, or by their nature, such as an old brick path and honeysuckle-covered rustic arch leading into a cottage garden. Of course you might decide to keep the garden a secret until the last minute by making the entrance via a solid oak door in a high brick wall, or else you could create a way in down a narrow gravel path, hemmed in by tall plants either side and overhanging trees before it turns a corner into a wide open, light and airy garden as a complete contrast.

Romantic entrance
Rosa *'Adelaide d'Orléans' smothers an archway leading into an informal country garden.*

Front entrances and garden gates

As with all garden design, simplicity and unity are the keynotes for the design of front entrances.
Their style needs to be in keeping with that of the house and any adjacent garden structures. A gate that matches a low picket fence will look in place and inviting, but a contrasting gate, say in black railings or solid wood set in a wall or thick prickly hedge, will make a much stronger 'keep out' statement, particularly if the gate happens to match the wall in height.

Welcoming garden gate
The open structure of this white gate set in a wall, the neat brick path and array of informal cottage plants — roses, delphiniums, hollyhocks and violas — sets a friendly tone.

Linking internal divisions

Your garden design may divide the garden, particularly if it is long and narrow or odd-shaped, into two or more separate spaces, each with their own boundaries.

A useful way of demarcating these areas is to use trellis, which screens without creating a totally enclosed feeling. The areas will need to be linked at some point, perhaps by an arch or gateway, which will allow the opportunity for contrast and similarity, secrecy and openness, to add yet another dimension to the garden.

Connecting arch
Looking through an arch of honeysuckle allows a glimpse of shrub roses and catmint, while the two garden areas are linked and unified by the continuous lawn surface.

Fences

Choice of fencing style and material depends partly on the purpose of the fence, partly on the design of the garden itself, and on cost. A 1.8m (6ft) high fence of posts with woven or lapped panels ensures complete privacy, for example, but may not be the most sympathetic backdrop to planting. A post and rail fence, to which vertical boards or palings are nailed, is a strong, attractive, but more costly partition.

Where privacy is not essential, the vertical boards may be spaced out (palisade or picket) or fixed at an angle (chevron), making the fence more economical and adding interest. These open fences (including trellis) are better for nearby plants as they allow air, light and rain onto them, as well as filtering the wind. Apart from timber, metal in the form of plain railings or wrought iron is extremely popular, and even plastic fences have their place.

Subtle partition
This simple yet attractive post and rail fence draws attention to the planting while allowing air and sunlight to filter through.

Trellis fences

To increase the height of an existing fence, or wall, either for privacy or security, you can use trellis fencing.

Made from lightweight timber battens, nailed in square or diamond patterns, it is the ideal solution for adding some extra height to an existing fence. Plants can then be grown against it, or,

indeed, twining climbers, such as honeysuckle, can be encouraged to grow through it, which will eventually more or less obscure the actual construction.

It pays to choose stoutly made trellis. Ideally, the timbers should be at least 2.5cm (1in) in section, and they should be treated with preservative. Trellis can be bought in ready-made panels, which are then nailed to the supporting structure, or it can be constructed by a carpenter to your own design. (It can also be used to screen parts of the garden, see p.47).

If you wish, you can stain or paint the trellis, which will help to preserve it. Soft colours, such as sage greens, dove greys and dusky blues, are the most successful.

Using trellis to extend a solid fence
A trellis supporting climbing plants is a compromise that ensures privacy while not cutting out too much light.

(It can also be used to screen parts of the garden, see p.47).

Erecting wooden fence posts

Set the posts in concrete, or use metal fence post supports. For most fencing, use 7.5cm (3in) square posts of pressure-treated timber. Coat the section to go into the ground with a bitumastic compound. To calculate the length of the posts, add 2.5cm (1in) to the height of the fence panels, allowing for any capping or base board, plus the length of post going into the ground, about 60cm (24in) if it is to be set in concrete. Mark the post 2.5cm (1in) from the top; mark the height from here of the fence panels and also ground level (if different from the bottom of panels).

Concreting in a post
Place a string marker along the ground on the forward edge of the fence line. Dig a hole 35cm (14in) square, so the string lies one-third the way across the hole. A layer of small stones will assist drainage, so make the hole about 6-8cm (2½-3in) deeper than required. Fill with mortar to 5cm (2in) below ground level, checking that the post is plumb with a spirit level. Compact the mortar and leave to set.

1 *Check the post's ground level marker is at the correct height and its forward edge lies against the string marker.*

2 *Infill with mortar, using a spirit level to keep post vertical and a strut to keep it in position while the concrete sets.*

Constructing a panel fence

With panel fencing, the panels are nailed to the posts while the mortar is still wet. Mark the top and bottom of the panel. The top should come 2.5cm (1in) below the top of the posts.

To measure between the posts, place a panel on the ground, on the string line of the fence and against the foot of the first upright post. Insert a stick in the ground where the centre of the second post front will be. Remove the panel, mark and dig out the hole for the post. Fill with mortar and insert the post.

To position the panel, tap nails horizontally into the inside edges of both posts at the lower (ground) marker and place the panel on the supporting nails. Check with a spirit level that the panel is level, and nail into position.

For a 1.5m (5ft) fence panel, five nails are used for fixing the panel: starting from the back of the panel, insert three evenly spaced nails at the top, centre and bottom and, from the front of the panel, insert two in between.

1 *Measure the distance of the first post from the second by laying the panel flat against the foot of the first upright post.*

2 *The panel lowered onto the supporting nails on the lower marker, and (inset) using 5cm (2in) nails to affix the panel.*

3 *A completed section of panel fence. Once the fence is in position, it will need an annual coat of preservative to protect it.*

Constructing a picket fence

Here the mortar is left to set overnight before the pickets or pales are fixed to the rails.

The post height should be that of the vertical pale *minus* the pointed tip, plus 60cm (24in) to be inserted into the ground. Once the first post is set in concrete, calculate the distance between the posts and thus the length of the crossrails, which should be at most 3m (10ft). The rails, 5cm (2in) wide and 2.5cm (1in) thick, overlap the endposts. Concrete in all the uprights (the two endposts first) using a string guide to ensure all the posts align correctly.

Mark the position of the upper rail, 12cm (5in) from the post top, and the lower, 15cm (6in) from the ground. Fix the upper rail (have someone hold the other end), and position it fully across the endpost and half-way across the in-between post. Repeat for the lower rail. Use nails (place diagonally for the end posts and horizontally for those in between) long enough to go 2.5cm (1in) into the posts. To affix the pales, secure a string guide between the tops of the endposts. Half insert nails in the first pale at the centre of the two crossrails. Hold the pointed top against the string and outer edge of the post, and hammer in the nails, checking the pale is vertical with a spirit level.

For the second pale, half insert the top nail, and, taking another pale as a spacer, place the two pales together against the first. Hammer nails into position. Repeat for the whole fence.

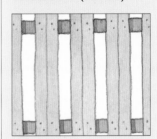

1 *Fixing the top rail to a post with two nails. The crossrails would overlap endposts completely.*

2 *Positioning a pale, showing the spacer pale used to determine the gap between pales.*

3 *The end post showing overlapping crossrail and pale. Use thinner spacers for greater privacy.*

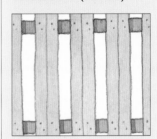
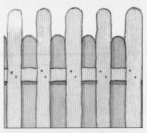

Hedges

To all intents and purposes, hedges are living walls or fences. They make just as good screens, and are often better as windbreaks and for blocking out noise. Formal hedges, almost always of a single variety, result from regular, close trimming, sometimes several times a year, to produce sharply defined straight lines or curves. For the more elaborate geometric shapes, small-leaved evergreen plants, such as yew (*Taxus baccata*) box (*Buxus sempervirens*), red cedar (*Thuja plicata*), privet (*Ligustrum*) and holly (*Ilex*), are best – but neat shapes can also be made from deciduous species, such as hawthorn (*Crataegus*), beech (*Fagus*) and hornbeam (*Carpinus*).

Informal hedges are trimmed infrequently, perhaps only once a year after flowering, and have a softer, more irregular outline. Berberis, cotoneaster, potentilla and roses are just some examples of suitable plants. For an attractive, and also traditional, hedgerow, you can mix different plant varieties, provided they are all roughly of the same vigour.

Formal hedging
Using a combination of tall and low hedging defines different areas in a formal garden. Here, a closely clipped yew (Taxus baccata) *hedge forms the backdrop to a chequerboard of box* (Buxus sempervirens).

Decorative hedging

If the effort of maintaining a formal, clipped hedge and even topiary shapes is not your particular hobby, there is a range of shrubby plants with fine leaf or flower colour, some of which are dense or prickly enough to put off possible two or four-footed intruders.

When selecting a plant variety for a hedge, make sure that its general growth rate and eventual height are compatible with the size of hedge you want to create. You will never achieve a 2-metre (6ft) high hedge with potentilla or hypericum because it is not capable of growing that tall. On the other hand, keeping a Leyland cypress (x *Cupressocyparis* spp.) at 50cm (20in) high would be like trying to stop a runaway train – you will be trimming it almost every week.

Alternating conifers
This unusual row makes a good backdrop for a perennial border.

Traditional box
The deserved favourite for formal low hedging for centuries.

Cheerful yellow flowers
Hypericum provides long-lasting colour in early summer.

Blazing berries and thorns
Autumn colour apart, pyracanthus makes an impenetrable barrier.

Rosa rugosa
Pink flowers are followed by huge hips lasting into late autumn.

Tapestry effect
For a country-style hedge, use two or more species mixed together.

Hedges and screens as dividers

Hedges are useful for dividing space within the garden as well as for boundaries. Most gardens, even small ones, benefit if the entire garden is not viewed in one glance. Different forms of hedging, and varying hedge heights, can be used for this purpose, as can various screening materials, such as trellis or bamboo.

For low-level hedges, box (*Buxus sempervirens*) is the most popular plant. It creates a dense, neat, evergreen hedge and, being slow-growing, needs infrequent clipping. Small flowering shrubs with small leaves, such as santolina and lavender, also make good low hedges. Larger screening can be created with taller hedges of yew or privet, whereas partial screening of a small area can be carried out with a 'hedge' of tall grasses or bamboos. Alternatively, trellis can be put up, through which plants, like clematis, honeysuckle or campis, are encouraged to twine.

It is important that the style of the hedge is in keeping with the design of the garden. Neatly clipped evergreens work well in small formal designs but they can also provide an effective backdrop to an informal border, providing a 'holding'

Dividing line
A clipped, low hedge separates areas of a large garden, allowing different design themes in each.

structure for the planting. Evergreen screening plants can be clipped into neat shapes to punctuate different areas in a formal garden.

Screening methods
Clipped shrubs act as small screening devices, lending an air of mystery to a small garden and making it appear larger than it is.

Planting a hedge

To look their best, hedges often need as much care, both in planting and subsequently, as most ornamental shrubs. Hedging plants are best bought small and in bulk. Once planted, keep the soil weed-free and water frequently during dry spells for at least the first season.

Conifer hedge
Mark the line of the hedge using canes and string (two canes for a straight hedge;

5 to 7 canes for a curve). Make a trench of well-worked soil, dug to at least 75cm (30in) depth, carefully forking out perennial weeds.

The trench should be made about 30cm (12in) wider overall than the expected hedge width. Dig as much well-rotted

Single row of conifers
To ensure an equal distance between the hedging plants, place a cane on the ground between the centres of the planting holes.

compost or organic matter into the lower spit of soil as you can. For even better results, sprinkle over and fork in slow-release or long term fertilizer before planting.

Conifers should be set in a single row at least 45–60cm (18–24in) apart (but 75cm/ 30in for Leyland cypress).

After placing the shrub in the hole, pack the root area with soil and gently firm in with the heel. Conifers do not need to be clipped after planting; simply clip lightly in the early years.

Deciduous hedge
For an impenetrable barrier, deciduous species are often planted in a double alternating row. Proceed as for planting conifers, but make the trench width the same as the intended hedge width.

Double row of deciduous plants
Allow 45cm (18in) between rows, and slightly more space between plants than for a single row. After planting clip back side shoots and the leader shoot by a third in late autumn.

Arches and pergolas

Pergolas and arches are desirable features to include in even the smallest garden. They create immediate height and vertical interest; they can frame a distant view of a statue, act as focal points themselves, or they divide a garden into spaces without the solidity of fences or hedges. Above all, they display plants.

A simple pergola can be turned into a cosy little arbour or sitting area by closing in three sides, perhaps with trellis panels covered with clematis and honeysuckle. Wood is a traditional material, whether simply sawn or extravagantly carved and moulded, but many other materials including metal, stone, brick and even light plastic-covered metal, can be used on their own or in combination. Brick and stone, for example, would be primarily used for building narrow columns or piers to support metal or wooden roof beams. All these materials have their own particular merits. Wood is relatively economical, whilst wrought iron, though more expensive, is tremendously flexible.

Arches and pergolas can be bought in kit form to create your own instant garden feature. But if you wanted something a little different from standard sizes and shapes, you would need either to make it yourself or have it tailor-made professionally.

A cool, airy pergola
Baskets of bright pink impatiens add a dash of colour to this all-green pergola. The greyish-green paint harmonizes well with the plants.

Ideal supports for plants

Pergolas and arches are ideal for a whole range of climbing plants. Vigorous, twining or self-clinging varieties such as honeysuckle (*Lonicera* spp.) and wisteria will quickly reach the top of the posts or columns with little help required. However, more delicate types like *Clematis alpina* or those with little or no ability to cling strongly, for example *Trachelospermum* may need some assistance at least to the top of any uprights.

Painted slender metal poles sometimes provide very little grip for climbers, which will continually slide down. In situations like this, some additional wires or strings wrapped around the uprights will provide that extra hold for the plants until they reach the top and can become self-supporting.

If you wish to create a shaded area of the garden, you can use a series of arches or pergolas to cover a path, or perhaps use two to make a shady bower over a seat. Fruiting vines can be grown over pergolas or arches to create shade, and provide edible crops.

A flowery tunnel
A rose arch is an eye-catching feature, particularly at the height of its flowering season. Arches do not have to be used singly: place three or four at regular intervals to create a light and airy 'tunnel' of roses.

Constructing pergola posts

The pergola shown here is constructed along a newly laid brick path. Spacing between the uprights is roughly equal to the width of the pergola. For example, whether the span across the path is 1m (3ft) as here, or 1.8m (6ft), the distance between the posts should be the same.

The height will depend to a large extent on use: a thoroughfare will need to be 2.5m (8ft), a decorative arch or arbour can be lower.

The end posts of the pergola are positioned first. Dig a hole for each based on a square of the post size (7.5cm/3in) and about 60cm (24in) deep. Each post should be set in cement in a 1:4 to 1:6 proportion of cement to combined aggregate in a stiff mix (see p.31). Once the endposts have been positioned guidelines (string or canes) should be run between their tops so that the posts in between are set at a common level.

Two people are needed to position the posts: one to fill the hole with cement and the other to hold a spirit level against the upright post. Once the cement is hard, the supports and crossbeams can be fixed (see below).

1 *Using a spirit level, check throughout the operation that the post is exactly upright, from all angles.*

2 *As it is fed into the hole, the concrete is tamped down with the shovel and smoothed off. Make sure that it slopes so that water runs away from the post.*

3 *A strut nailed to the post at an angle keeps it in position until the concrete sets. A final smoothing off of the cement mix can be done with a metal tamp.*

Arch and pergola roofs

The fundamental structure of arches and pergolas doesn't vary, and in its simplest form consists of upright posts or columns linked together across their tops usually with horizontal rails or beams. So the simplest arch might just consist of two rustic poles set upright in the ground, joined across the top with a third pole nailed into place. From this starting point, all pergolas and tunnels evolve.

Crossbeams set flush
Supports and crossbeams are half-jointed, so they interlock fully. Here the support sits in a joist hanger attached to a wall.

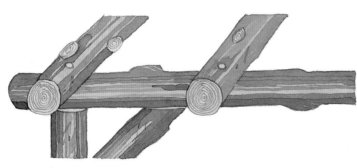

Round rustic poles
The simplest roof with poles nailed together. Using untreated wood means that this arch's life will be short – however, the poles are fairly easily replaced.

Raised crossbeams
Only the crossbeams are cut, so they sit higher than the support beams. The beam ends are shaped as a small detail.

Plants for pergolas and arches

These are just some of the many plants suitable for pergolas or other structures. Most have been chosen for their scent as well as for their flowers.

Actinidia kolomikta
Akebia quinata
Bougainvillea (B. glabra)

Clematis (C. alpina, C. armandii, C. x durandii, C. 'Gypsy Queen' and other large-flowered cvs, C. montana 'Elizabeth', C. x macropetala, C. viticella)
Golden hop (Humulus lupulus 'Aureus')
Honeysuckle (Lonicera x americana, L. caprifolium,

L. periclymenum)
L. x tellmanniana)
Itea (I. ilicifolia)
Jasmine (Jasminum nudiflorum, J. officinale)
Laburnum x waterei
Passionflower (Passiflora caerulea, P.c. 'Constance Elliott')
Rose (many Rosa spp., e.g. 'Golden Showers', 'Madame Grégoire Staechelin', 'Spanish

Beauty', 'Mermaid', 'Morning Jewel, 'New Dawn')
Solanum crispum
Sweet pea (Lathyrus odoratus)
Tropaeolum speciosum, T. tuberosum
Vitis coignetiae, V. vinifera 'Purpurea'
Wisteria (W. floribunda, W. sinensis)

Water features

There can be very few gardens that would not be enhanced by the addition of a small pool or water feature. Indeed in hot, dry climates where water is a valued resource, such features have often been central to garden design. The style of your chosen water feature should reflect the nature of your garden. Circular and square ponds are in keeping with formal features, while irregular shaped ponds and meandering streams might be more in keeping with wild or informal gardens.

The essence of any water feature, of course, is that it must hold an amount of water suitable for its intended purpose without leaking, or at least not noticeably, and this principle applies from the tiniest half-barrel pool to the largest lake.

Flowing or moving water is easily achieved by means of submersible pumps which can be used to create spouts or fountains, or else to carry water to a higher level from which it can return to the pool or other feature via a waterfall, stream or cascade.

Striking a balance
The strong architecture of this house is balanced by a formal, circular pool close by. The curved slabs of the pool's edge reflect the material used to pave the patio, serving as a link between house and garden.

Containing water

Though the traditional method of lining ponds with puddled clay still has its place, for the average garden owner there are other ways to create a water feature, whether for still or moving water:
• By lining a suitably prepared excavation with a flexible polythene, PVC or rubber-based liner.
• Using pre-formed ponds, usually made from fibreglass or plastic, or other rigid containers such as wood, metal and stone.
• Making a strong concrete shell rendered with waterproofed mortar.
• To provide a flexible waterproof layer, using *in-situ* fibreglass applied to a concrete or brick shell.
The first two methods are by far the most popular, partly by virtue of their relatively modest cost, and partly because only a modest degree of skill is required. The first method (see opposite) is also best for small features, such as bubble fountains.

Miniature fountain
The focal point of this courtyard garden is a pool and fountain enclosed by a raised brick edge and surrounding planting.

Trough with wall spout
Moving water transforms a solid stone trough into a delightful water feature. A low-power submersible pump, with careful concealment of the supply hose and wiring, is all that's required.

Wooden half barrel
This makes a perfectly adequate place for planting miniature waterlilies, which prefer still water, and rushes (here Nymphaea tetragona and Typha minima).

Making a lined pond

Flexible liners come in a range of materials and sizes, with cheaper PVC and polythene best suited to simple features. The heaviest-duty liners are used for reservoirs! In deciding the pond shape, remember it is easier to have shallow curves and gently sloping sides to avoid making large folds in the liner.

For marking out the pond you will need a supply of short canes, string and a datum peg (roughly as long as the pond depth – see p.29), marked 2.5cm (1in) from its top. Also mark a few short pegs in the same way.

Insert the datum peg near the centre of the pond area, so that the mark is at ground level. Place levelling pegs about 30cm (1ft) outside the pond circumference, using a spirit level from the datum peg to each in turn. In this way you can check that the sides are to a uniform level.

Excavate to one spade depth (spit) across the pond area. Dig out a second spit, and so on, until the required depth and shape are reached. To check the depth, remove the datum peg, place a straight edge above the hole, between two levelling pegs, and measure down.

Before installing the liner, remove all stones and roots.

Flatten the ground and line the bottom, sides and shelf with a layer of sand. Centre the liner over the pond and gently lower it in position, until it just touches the pond base. Hold the liner edges loosely in place with bricks or stones. Gradually fill the pond with water, easing the liner into place and making folds as you go. Once the liner is seen to be level all round – so no water spills – remove the holding stones.

1 Use a spirit level to check that all levelling pegs outside the pond circumference are at the same height as the datum peg.

2 The pond is dug out to second spit depth; note the 30cm (12in) flat shelf left for marginal, shallow-water plants.

3 Line the sides, shelf and base with a 3-5cm (1-3in) layer of moist soft sand and level with a wooden float.

4 Lower the liner into position, using stones or bricks to secure edges. Fill with water, making folds in the liner as you go.

5 Position edging stones and trim the liner to 30cm (12in). Taking each slab in turn, tamp gently into position on a pad of mortar, using a 1:4 cement: soft sand mix. Point several slabs at a time.

The finished pond
In a short time the pond is transformed with marginal plants, waterlilies and pond edge planting. To secure and conceal the pond liner, you can use any type of paving material – as long as it reflects the style of the garden. The paving slabs should slightly overlap the pond edge. Cover the pond bottom and shelf with 3cm (1in) topsoil to help stabilize the water temperature, assist bacterial activity (if fish are to be kept in the pond), and provide nutrients for plants to grow.

Calculating pond liner size

The major cost of the pond is the liner, so it is vital to work out how much liner you will need at the outset. Use four pegs to mark the *maximum* length and width of your proposed pond, be it a rectangle or an irregular shape.

liner width = max. pond width + (max. depth x 2)

liner length = max. pond length + (max. depth x 2)

The pond illustrated is 1.5m wide x 2.2m long x 0.75m deep, therefore:

liner width = 1.5m + (0.75m x 2) = 3m

liner length = 2.2m + (0.75m x 2) = 3.7m

Containers

Containers are the ideal solution for small-space gardening, permitting you to grow a surprisingly wide range of plants on patios, balconies, roof terraces and in window boxes and to group the displays successfully. Choosing an appropriate form and size of container is a key element in successful container gardening. The range of terracotta pots is now vast, and you can find almost any shape or size to suit your needs.

One of the great benefits of container gardening is that it allows you to move the plants around, so that those in flower are in the foreground and those out of flower are out of sight. Another bonus is that you can grow plants in specialized conditions, such as an acid-loving azalea in a pot of ericaceous compost. However, containers do need more attention than conventionally planted gardens, because they dry out so quickly and need frequent watering. You also need to provide nutrients for the plants on a regular basis, and repot the plants as they grow.

Creating a colourful environment
A small paved garden and timber-decked terrace is brought to life with the addition of a variety of containers. Vibrant greenery and interesting foliage are teamed with blue, lilac and yellow flowers.

Wall displays

In small gardens it pays to use the wall space as well as the floor space for planting. Groups of matching pots can be fixed to the wall on brackets or trellis to create vividly colourful displays on an otherwise blank canvas.

This is particularly useful for walls alongside narrow alleys which get very little light at the foot of the wall, narrowing the range of what

you can grow. If you repeat a theme in several pots, it will give the area both visual interest and a strong sense of design unity. Many small flowering plants are ideal for this purpose, and you can replant the containers to give a year-long display.

Wall flowers
Small terracotta pots filled with blue pansies hang on a trellis-clad wall, with matching lavender in rectangular pots on top.

Planting a wall pot
1 *Place some stones for drainage at the base of the pot. Half fill the pot with compost and insert the first plant.*

2 *Fill with remaining plants, add compost to within 3cm (1in) of the rim and water well. Fix the pot to the wall.*

Free-standing containers

The choice of materials for containers is wonderfully varied, from simple unadorned terracotta to delicate and ornate wire. It is important to theme your containers in some way, either by colour or material, to prevent the display developing an unattractively 'bitty' look.

Make sure you have some big containers, perhaps containing one handsome feature plant, such as cordyline or a small tree. Square wooden tubs, known as 'Versailles' tubs, are ideal for formal displays of clipped box, often used in matching pairs either side of a doorway or flight of steps.

Window boxes can be of painted wood or terracotta, and you can create displays with, say, two round pots either side of a long rectangular area for greater visual interest, and to give some variety in the planting theme. Objects not intended as plant containers will sometimes serve the purpose very well, including old chimney pots, sinks or even wheelbarrows. Oil drums and plastic containers can be given a coat of paint and are surprisingly effective. Make sure any 'found' container has drainage holes created in the base, and use a layer of stones at the bottom to ensure the holes do not block with compost. Repot most plants every two years.

Wooden containers
Containers made of wood, even durable timber such as English oak, are best treated inside and underneath with a preservative – check that it is suitable for use near plants though.

Stone containers
Generally these need no treatment and can be planted straightaway. Be wary, however, of planting lime-hating plants, such as camellias or rhododendrons, in concrete tubs unless they are sealed inside, due to the presence of lime in the concrete.

Metal containers
Metals like iron and steel will rust, so may need treatment. So that the soil does not become contaminated by metals such as zinc or lead, found in antique or reproduction containers, paint the insides with latex-based paint or line them with heavy polythene.

Hanging baskets

For small spaces nothing beats a hanging basket as a show stopper since it is seen alone, and in the round. Some wonderfully vibrant displays can be achieved in baskets, but they do require very frequent watering since their exposure to drying winds causes moisture to evaporate rapidly. As with other container plantings, you could mix water-retentive granules with the compost. This will keep it moist for longer, although at the height of summer, daily watering is still essential, especially if the basket hangs in full sun. Feeding throughout the growing season is also a priority. Some slow-release fertilizer added to the compost when you plant the basket in late spring should supply the necessary nutrients. Hanging baskets look most effective if they have a limited colour scheme, either toning colours, two contrasting colours or a single colour. Any small trailing foliage or flowering plants can be used. Trailing forms of petunia, pelargonium, lobelia, nasturtium and ivy are popular.

Double the impact
When planting hanging baskets, sticking to a theme of just one or two colours often produces the best results, as these stunning displays of Pelargonium *and* Lobelia *demonstrate.*

Planting a hanging basket
1 *Place moss around the sides of the basket and then line it with a pierced plastic liner. Half-fill the basket with compost.*

2 *Start to add the plants, pushing some of them into the sides so that the whole basket is eventually covered.*

Structural planting

Structural planting is a phrase that often appears in discussions of garden design, and while it is a vital aspect to consider when planning a garden, it is actually quite difficult to define in precise terms. In essence, though, it could be described as a permanent framework of woody plants, that is to say trees and shrubs, which can be infilled with other smaller plants such as perennials, bulbs and grasses, and which results in a cohesive effect at all times of the year. Without such framework planting, most gardens would be very bitty and fragmented. At the same time, these trees and shrubs are used as one would use man-made garden features, to frame views, screen, divide or act as focal points. So the actual locations of trees and larger shrubs become more than just positions where they can be seen and appreciated as individual items of beauty: they are an intrinsic part of the garden design or scheme.

Some shrubs will assume almost tree-like proportions, which can be an advantage if your tree choice is otherwise limited, particularly in small gardens. Many large shrubs have distinctive growth habits, such as *Kerria japonica* 'Pleniflora' which is tall and upright, or *Viburnum plicatum* 'Mariesii', which is wide and spreading. Knowledge of plants' growth habits can be used to help you select shrubs, and indeed trees, that will serve a particular purpose in the framework of your garden.

Foliage composition
Here, trees and shrubs provide structure with dense evergreens giving contrasts of colour and height. The deciduous foreground trees will allow sunlight to filter through.

Tree and shrub forms
The natural form that trees and shrubs take creates a very positive design statement. The variation in these forms can be used to great effect in any design.

Small gardens, in particular, will benefit from the naturally columnar or conical shape of some trees, cypresses and conifers, for example. A small weeping tree is ideal as a focal point in a small formal garden. The forms of shrubs are equally varied. The tall sword-like leaves of yuccas and cordylines make a strong architectural statement, and, in handsome containers,

these make ideal punctuation plants to mark a transition in the design from one area to another. Shrubs with a spreading growth habit such as some cotoneasters and junipers, are useful where there are changes of level in the garden. A selection of some of the more popular forms of tree and shrub are shown right.

Try to suit the shape to the purpose. Columnar trees are ideal for small spaces while those with rounded canopies will help create areas of shade. When choosing shrubs, try to select as many different forms as possible to add interest to the planting.

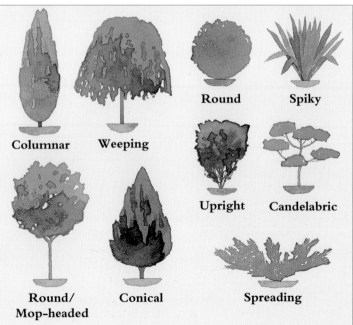

Columnar   Weeping   Round   Spiky

Round/Mop-headed   Conical   Upright   Candelabric   Spreading

Large-scale structure

Any garden will benefit from having a tree or two to provide vertical interest, and even quite small gardens can have at least two or three small trees or large shrubs.

Try to pick different forms, and a mixture of evergreen and deciduous types. Foliage colour and shape is important, too, and there are numerous colours and textures to choose from. Even the bare branches of deciduous trees add substance to the garden framework.

Because of their scale, trees assume probably the most important role in a garden and siting them carefully is critical. Avoid planting all the trees around the perimeter, and try to position one small tree as a focal point. Japanese maples are excellent feature trees for small gardens, and many have excellent autumn colour as well.

While evergreen trees are useful for year-round effect, remember that in the shorter days of winter, they may cast heavy shadows.

Tropical atmosphere
Palms, here surrounded by ferns and cordyline, *can look very exotic when lit up at night.*

Small-scale structure

Shrubs provide the next level of the planting scheme, which the smaller perennials and annuals flesh out. Make sure that the shrubs have an interesting form. Many small-leaved evergreens that do not make naturally good shapes can be clipped or pruned to improve on nature.

It is a good idea to have a mixture of forms and foliage types in the garden. Look for varieties with interestingly marked foliage – many have gold or silver variegated leaves which will 'lighten' the effect of very dense foliage. At a lower level, mound-forming shrubs can be used to provide weed-suppressing ground cover. Heathers are particularly useful for this purpose. Aim to have a mixture of evergreen and deciduous shrubs – you will probably need one evergreen variety for every two or three deciduous ones to achieve a reasonable balance.

Bamboos and grasses
Tall bamboo above a low trickle fountain provides a focal point at the end of the path, its shape echoed by surrounding smaller clumps of grasses.

Foliage interest

Gardens need not be in flower to look good, and provided there is ample variety of form and foliage colour, will look interesting all year round.

Aim for a mixture of textures and leaf forms. Grasses, with their slender, often arching, leaves make a good contrast to the more typical oval leaf forms, throwing these into relief. In small gardens, a sense of unity can be created by concentrating on foliage rather than flowers, the colour being kept largely to one part of the garden, perhaps in a changing display of container plants. Remember, too, that there are many differently coloured leaves, not simply green. Plants with gold, purple and silver- and gold-variegation are worth looking out for and many plants turn attractive shades of scarlet, russet and gold in the autumn. Leaf shapes can vary from large hand-shaped leaves to neat ovals. Use plants with a wide range of attributes for the most interesting effects.

Contrasting foliage
The varied colours, textures and shapes of Salvia, Digitalis, *grasses and* Carpinus *work well together in a small garden.*

Trained ivy
A simple terracotta pot with variegated ivy – in this case trained in a spiral over wire – can act as a focal point.

Designing borders

Almost every gardener's dream is to create a brilliantly coloured border or bed for their garden, but orchestrating the whole is a complex task that requires a great deal of diligent research into plant sizes, flowering times and colour. The task is made more difficult if you wish to create a border or bed that looks good all year round. Generally, a mixed shrub and perennial border is easier to get right than a border made up solely of perennial plants, although the latter tend to give a more brilliant effect during a short season of the year. The greatest perennial borders are usually renowned for the season in which they are at their best – normally spring, summer or autumn. If you are fortunate in having a larger garden, you might plant up one border for spring, another for summer and a third for autumn.

Summer colour
Poppies (Papaver orientalis)*, Sambucus nigra and Spiraea japonica 'Goldflame' provide shades of red, orange and yellow that give this traditional summer mixed border a 'hot' colour theme.*

Shrub border for partial shade

Areas of the garden in partial shade are usually best given over to shrub borders, since there is a wide choice of shrubs that will do well in some shade, whereas many perennials prefer full sun.

The aim in a shrub border is to get a good mixture of foliage colours and textures, so the border looks attractive even when the shrubs are not in flower. A combination of evergreen and deciduous shrubs is normally the most effective, providing a shape and structure to the border even during the winter.

This predominantly shrub border features a few herbaceous perennials to give it variety and a little extra pace and colour – a geranium for a splash of lavender-blue in

mid-summer, and rudbeckias for yellow highlights in late summer. The shrubs include a couple to add scent – the philadelphus and elaeagnus – plus a berberis for some purple-red contrast.

Colour and form
The colour scheme in this border is one of golds, purples, rusty oranges and blues. Foliage colour and form plays and important part, providing interest through most of the year.

Plant list
The shrubs are all planted singly; perennials that act as infill in groups of three or five, according to size.
1 *Cotoneaster frigidus*
2 *Miscanthus sinensis* (such as 'Silver Feather' or another similar grass)
3 *Fuchsia riccartonii*
4 *Buddleja davidii* 'Black Knight' (deep purple flowers)
5 *Elaeagnus x ebbingei* 'Limelight'
6 *Philadelphus* 'Belle Etoile'
7 *Juniperus x media* 'Mint Julep'
8 *Hydrangea quercifolia* 'Snow Queen'
9 *Potentilla* 'Goldfinger'
10 *Spiraea* 'Goldflame'
11 *Berberis* 'Dart's Red Lady'
12 *Rudbeckia* 'Goldsturm'
13 *Weigela florida*
14 *Carex morrowii* 'Evergold'
15 *Acanthus spinosus*
16 *Geranium* 'Johnson's Blue'
17 *Thuja* 'Smaragd' (or similar small conical evergreen)
18 *Euonymus* 'Emerald 'n' Gold'

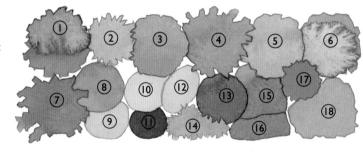

Perennial border for full sun

A thriving perennial border in summer or autumn is something that all keen plantspeople hanker after.

The planning of such a border in terms of the heights and flowering times of the plants is very tricky. You also need some colour sense to make the finished result attractive.

If in doubt, go for a single colour (yellow or white are popular), or pick a range of pastels (pinks, mauves, blues and whites) or strong contrasts (yellows, oranges, purples and blues).

In this border, colour is introduced not just in the bright flower colours, such as the yellows of rudbeckias and the rusty oranges of heleniums, but in strong foliage colour too, for example the purple-tinged *Salvia officinalis* 'Purpurescens' and reddish purple *Sedum telephium*. A couple of shrubs, such as hydrangeas and euonymus, could also be added to help to give the border structure.

Summer brights

Purples, oranges, blues, yellows and whites make a vibrant mix in this exuberant and colourful sunny border. Foliage interest is provided by the likes of Carex striata *and* Festuca glauca.

Plant list
1 *Rudbeckia* 'Goldsturm'
2 *Deschampsia* spp. or *Carex striata*
3 Hybrid *Delphinium*
4 Bronze-flowered *Helenium* (such as *H.* 'Coppelia')
5 *Phlox paniculata* (such as *P.p.* 'Marlborough')
6 *Echinops ritro*
7 *Leucanthemum maximum* (such as 'Wirral Supreme')
8 *Sedum telephium*
9 *Salvia uliginosa*
10 *Gaillardia*
11 *Iris sibirica*
12 *Euphorbia griffithii* 'Fireglow'
13 *Aster amellus* 'Vanity'
14 *Hemerocallis* spp.
15 *Erysimum* spp.
16 *Helichrysum* spp.
17 *Penstemon* such as 'Sour Grapes'
18 *Coreopsis verticillata*
19 *Hemerocallis* 'Hyperion'
20 *Festuca glauca*
21 *Geranium magnificum*
22 *Salvia officinalis* 'Purpurascens'

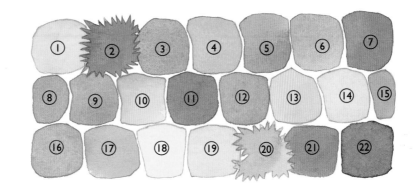

Spring borders

With their power to make us forget the starkness and cold of winter, the combination of spring-flowering shrubs and perennials with bulbs and corms is one of the delights of the garden. Whole beds can be filled with massed tulips and toning pansies, or with tulips and contrasting wallflowers. For a less labour-intensive display, you could try naturalizing grape hyacinths, squill and glory-of-the-snow.

The range of spring-flowering plants is huge, catering to any size of garden, any aspect and any colour scheme.

For shrubs and perennials, choose from forsythia, witch hazel, magnolias, rhododendrons, camellias and lilac, or from hellebores, bergenias, aubrietas and alyssums. Add to these the regular standbys such as daffodils, narcissi, tulips, muscari, and crocuses, or the more unusual fritillaries or erythroniums, and you can have borders that will look good from early spring until May. Also, because bulbs and corms vanish underground after flowering and can be over-planted with later-flowering perennials, you have the bonus of being able to double the usefulness of your border.

Traditional favourites
Narcissi, euphorbia, 'China Pink' tulips and geraniums mix in a traditional spring border.

On the wild side
'Spring Green' tulips and hyacinths are planted in a less formal arrangement.

Designing island beds

Although you can have borders composed entirely of shrubs, most people prefer to mix them with flowering plants for a more colourful and interesting display at any one time. Shrubs provide the backdrop for borders planted against boundary walls and form the centrepoint of the border if it is an 'island' bed – or one that you can walk right round. As a rule, an island bed should have a slightly asymmetric look, with the tallest plant slightly off-centre to avoid too 'bun-like' an appearance. Evergreens, like small conifers, or sword shaped plants, like cordylines, are good for providing this central backbone. Follow with medium-sized shrubs, scaling down towards sub-shrubs and tall perennials, with smaller perennials at the front of the border.

Individual displays
A lawn studded with several island beds provides a good opportunity to experiment with different plantings, as each bed is self-contained.

Creating a raised island bed

A small raised bed built as a retaining wall, or against an existing wall or freestanding, as here, is most useful, especially in a small patio garden.

This raised bed is built of an inner wall of cinder blocks and an outer wall of hand-made bricks, with a small gap in between (the width of the wall equals the length of a brick). The footing is 30cm (12in) wide, slightly wider than the wall, and 30cm (12in) deep. Using canes and string, mark out the site of the raised bed.

Calculate the width of the footing according to the width of the walling: here, one cinder block for the inner wall plus one hand-made brick for the outer = 23 cm (9in). Add 3.5cm (1^1/$_2$in) either side of the wall; total width 30cm (12in). Once the outside structure is complete, fill the base with stones or other drainage material to a depth of 3in (8cm) and fill with good garden soil or compost. (Acid-loving plants can be grown in a garden with alkaline soil by filling a raised bed with acid compost).

On a different level
Planting in and around a brick raised bed makes it a distinctive feature in the garden.

1 *The trench marked out with canes and string, with concrete footing in place. Leave to set overnight.*

2 *Building the inner cinder brick wall: each block is laid on a 10mm (^{1}/$_4$in) layer of mortar, with one end 'buttered' with a triangular dab of mortar.*

3 *Lay each corner of the outer wall, then construct outwards. After three or four courses, set a string guideline between each corner. Infill with bricks, inserting a butterfly tie at intervals to bond inner and outer walls.*

4 *The wall is finished with a course of coping bricks laid lengthways across the inner and outer walls.*

Design for an all-seasons island bed

The prominent position of an island bed demands that it look good all year round, and it is of key importance to create a planting plan that takes this into account. What you sacrifice in impact during one specific season, you gain in all-year-round value. It is important, therefore, that you pick your plants with care for maximum show – ideally they should have flower colour in one season, and perhaps offer good autumn leaf colour or attractive seedheads in another. The use of spring- and autumn-flowering bulbs – tulips, narcissi, autumn-flowering crocuses – extends the season further, and these have the advantage of not taking up a lot of space. As they die down, their foliage will be concealed by the herbaceous perennials. Finally, a few evergreens are also necessary, to ensure that the planting retains some of its shape in winter. When choosing your plants, remember too that they will be viewed from all sides. Plants of varying heights with an even growth habit will give the best effect.

Plant list

Large-feature plants are planted singly, smaller plants in groups of three or five, depending on size.

1 *Festuca glauca*
2 *Doronicum orientale* 'Spring Bouquet'
3 *Aster novi-belgii* 'Jenny'
4 *Phlox paniculata* ('Fujiyama')
5 *Phlox* 'David'
6 *Tulipa* 'White Triumphator'
7 *Hemerocallis* 'Pink Damask'
8 *Stipa gigantea*
9 *Penstemon* 'Sour Grapes'
10 *Juniper chinensis* 'Pyramidalis'
11 *Geranium phaeum*
12 New Zealand flax (*Phormium* spp.)
13 *Agapanthus* 'Bressingham Blue'
14 *Euphorbia amygdaloides*
15 *Coreopsis* 'Moonbeam'
16 *Hosta* 'Halcyon'
17 *Artemisia* 'Lambrook Silver'
18 *Scabiosa caucasia* 'Butterfly Blue'
19 *Liatris spicata*
20 *Iris pallida* 'Argentea Variegata'
21 *Helleborus orientalis* 'Heartsease'
22 *Alchemilla mollis*
23 *Berberis thunbergii atropurpurea*

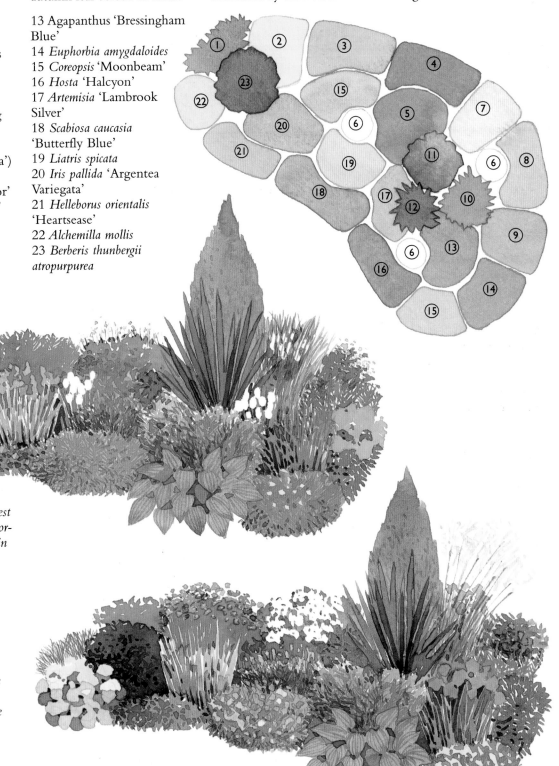

Island bed in spring
With a wealth of foliage interest (including juniper, berberis, phormium, festuca and euphorbia) in winter, colour is added in spring with tulips, doronicum and hellebores.

Island bed in summer
By summer the bed is in full swing, as the scabious (Scabiosa), penstemons, irises geraniums, asters and phlox come into flower. An attractive mix of foliage helps to flesh out the planting with hostas and alchemilla.

Design for pond-side planting

Water is a great asset in any garden. You can take advantage of a damp area to grow plants especially suited to moist soil and so create plantings in the form of a bog garden, with or without a pond.

Some of the most handsome plants come from moist soils and climates, their large lush leaves making a valuable contribution to any garden, as well as providing a respite from busy flower colour. Plants to use include ornamental rhubarb, large-leaved rodgersias, some of the big-leaved hostas and bamboos. It is a good idea to create the planting at one edge of the pond, rather than scattering it around the edges. Grouping the plants creates a more lush look to the pond, and the effect is more natural. If the pond is deep enough, include at least one floating aquatic (they require 90cm/3ft of water).

Bog garden
A damp area can be made to look very lush, with touches of colour from moisture-loving plants such as primulas and iris.

Plant list
Planted in groups of three, except *Glyceria* (1) and *Aponogeton* (1)
1. *Glyceria maxima* 'Variegata'
2 *Polygonum bistorta*
'Superbum'
3 *Rodgersia podophylla*
4 *Iris sibirica* 'Persimmon'
5 *Hosta* 'Francee'
6 *Astilbe* 'Elizabeth Bloom'
7 *Aponogeton distachyos*

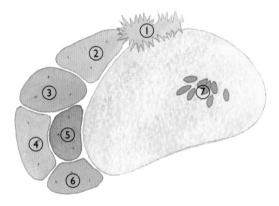

Leafy pond edges
Concentrate the marginal and poolside planting at one end of the pond for the best effect. Good foliage plants include Glyceria maxima.

Design for damp, shady corners

Many gardens have a damp, boggy area, often shaded by trees. There are a number of handsome foliage plants such as hostas and grasses that do well in these conditions and would create a small area of considerable planting interest. Damp shade also suits peat-loving plants like rhododendrons and ferns as well as plants like *Cimicifuga simplex* that dislike full sun. Other flowering perennials for damp shade are some of the euphorbias, monkshood (*Aconitum*), polygonum, thalictrum and veratrum.

Cool, shady group
This little group of perennials, ferns, grasses and shrubs all enjoy damp shade. Many shade plants have white flowers, creating a predominantly cool green and white colour scheme.

Plant list
Planted in groups of three, except for the hydrangea (1).
1 *Carex elatior* 'Aurea'
2. *Anemone japonica* 'Louise Whink'
3. *Hydrangea quercifolia*
4. *Hosta* 'Frances Williams'
5. *Polystichum setiferum*
6. *Polygonum amplexicaule atrosanguineum*

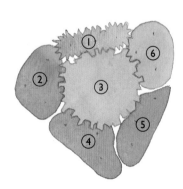

Design for dry, sunny borders

The plants for dry sunny conditions are often highly colourful, many of them with small silvery leaves that withstand drought conditions better than the larger, lusher leaves most often found in moisture-loving plants.

Big thistles do well in these conditions, as do the silver-leaved perennials such as lamb's ears (*Stachys byzantina* spp.), wormwood (*Artemisia* spp.) and senecio. Many geraniums, helianthemums and helichrysums, do well in hot sun, as do dianthus, hebe and small forms of phlox and penstemon. Try to aim for a good balance between large, medium and small perennials that like sunny conditions, and limit the theme to two colours (or toning colours), to give the area a feeling of unity.

Sun worshippers
Astromeria ligtu, Genista aetnensis *and* Lychnis *provide vibrant colour in a dry border.*

Plant list
Planted in groups of three, except for *Cistus (1)* and *Yucca (1)*.
1 *Eryngium* x *oliverianum*
2 *Cistus* x *purpureus*
3 *Hemerocallis hyperion*
4 *Euphorbia amygdaloides* 'Rubra'
5 *Yucca filamentosa*
6 *Aster ameleus* 'Violet Queen'

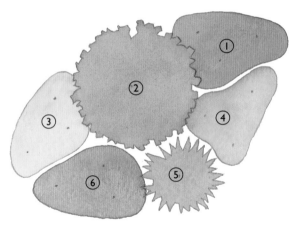

Mediterranean corner
This corner features plants that enjoy hot, sunny conditions. The yucca provides structure while the cistus counterbalances its form with brilliant flower colour.

Design for dry, shady corners

Dry shade is a common problem in small gardens with high walls, where the soil at the foot of the wall lies in the rain shadow area. It can be difficult to deal with this situation unless you turn to plants that naturally cope with dry shade. Among the larger plants that do well are foxgloves, alchemilla, pulmonarias and hellebores.

Dry, shady group
*Good foliage plants that cope well with dry shade include the attractively variegated euonymus and ground-covering bugle (*Ajuga reptans*).*

Plant list
Planted in groups of three, except mahonia (1).
1. *Dryopteris filix-mas*
2 *Euonymus* 'Emerald 'n' Gold'
3 *Mahonia* 'Charity'
4 *Ajuga reptans* 'Catlin's Giant'
5 *Iris foetidissima* 'Carina'
6 *Alchemilla mollis*

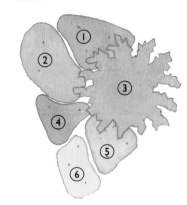

Planting designs for small spaces

If you have limited space, you are probably going to need to plant in containers and even if your garden is large, there will be areas, such as a patio, which will benefit from the occasional group of plants in pots. The aim in design terms is much the same as when planning larger borders and beds. Try to use foliage as well as flowers to create an impact, but ensure that the containers you choose are well suited to the plants, and enhance their attributes and qualities. It will pay to group the containers for maximum impact.

Many plants will do as well in containers as in the ground, but in their limited circumstances will demand a greater amount of care. They dry out notoriously quickly and need to be supplied with regular food and water. Most will also need repotting (depending on how vigorous they are) at least every two years.

Roof garden
A rooftop is lined with containers of plants on different levels, such as Rosa 'Scneewittchen and umbrella bamboo (Fargesia murieliae).

Design for a balcony

On a balcony, you usually need to get the most from a very limited space, so avoid plants with a spreading habit and go instead for conical plants, or those that will trail attractively over the edge of a wall or railing.

Make the most of the wall space for climbers, and try to leave an area free for a chair or two, or a small table. Placing a cluster of pots at one end looks better than scattering them randomly. The planting scheme here could be extended or reduced, depending on the size of the balcony. It has a mixture of architectural plants (bamboos and phormium), climbers (clematis and akebia), an evergreen shrub or two (*Choisya ternata* and *juniperus*) and colourful perennials. Including scented plants, like the lavender (*Lavandula angustifolia*), is also a good idea.

Plant list
These are all planted singly, except lavender (*Lavandula*), which has five plants to a trough, agapanthus (3) and sedum (3).
1 *Pleioblastus auricomus*
2 *Akebia quinata*
3 *Choisya ternata*
4 *Rosa* 'Happy Child'
5 *Helichrysum angustifolium*
6 *Solanum crispum*
7 *Agapanthus* 'Headbourne Hybrids'
8 *Fuchsia* 'Mrs Popple'
9 *Sedum* 'Vera Jameson'
10 *Hedera helix* 'Glacier'
11 *Lavandula angustifolia* 'Hidcote'
12 *Juniperus virginiana* 'Sulphur Spray'
13 *Clematis* 'Gipsy Queen'
14 *Phormium tenax purpureum*
15 *Akebia quinata*
16 *Hebe* 'Midsummer Beauty'
17 *Hosta* 'Halcyon'

A year-round balcony
A combination of perennials grown in pots, troughs and up a trellis provides year-round interest requiring little maintenance for a sheltered balcony.

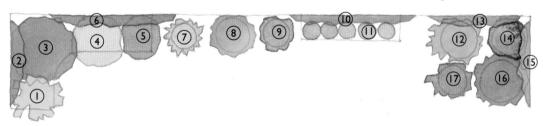

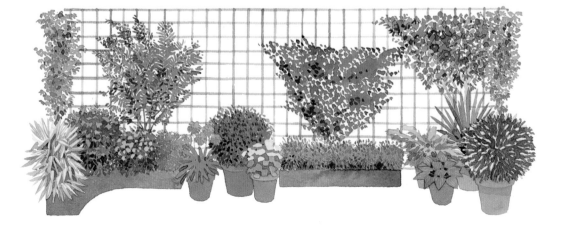

Designs for roof gardens

For a roof garden or small patio, you should concentrate the planting around the edges to leave space for seating and perhaps a table. A good mixture of evergreens for shelter, flowering shrubs and perennials for colour, and climbers and trailers is important, and plants included must be able to cope with the dry, sunny conditions of most patios and roof gardens. A good variety of container sizes and shapes widens the scope of your planting.

Plant list

1 *Campanula portenschlagiana*
2 *Pleioblastus auricomus*
3 *Clematis macropetala*
4 *Choisya* 'Aztec Pearl'
5 *Anthemis cupiana*
6 *Weigela* 'Victoria'
7 *Clematis* 'Gipsy Queen'
8 *Agapanthus* Headbourne Hybrids
9 *Juniperus* 'Sulphur Spray'
10 *Sedum* spp.
11 *Fuchsia* 'Mrs Popple'
12 *Rosa'*
13 *Phormium tenax purpureum*
14 *Salvia officinalis* 'Purpurascens'
15 *Elaeagnus ebbingei*
16 *Choisya* 'Sundance'
17 *Parthenocissus tricuspidata*
18 *Thuja plicata* 'Atrovirens'
19 *Ceanothus* 'Blue Mound'
20 *Hedera helix* 'Glacier'
21 *Thuja plicata* 'Atrovirens'
22 *Juniperus* 'Gold Sovereign'
23 *Parthenocissus tricuspidata*
24 *Philadelphus* 'Belle Etoile'
25 *Humulus lupus* 'Aureus'
26 *Hebe* 'Mrs Winder'
27 *Helichrysum angustifolium*
28 *Lonicera* x *americana*
29 *Potentilla fruticosa* 'Kobold'
30 *Aster* 'Violet Queen'
31 *Rosa* 'Evelyn'
32 *Stipa calamagrostis*
33 *Akebia quinata*
34 *Hydrangea quercifolia* 'Snow Queen'
35 *Campanula portenschlagiana*

A rooftop haven

This formally arranged combination of containers leaves plenty of room for a table and chairs or just for seating, so the owner can make the most of the sunshine.

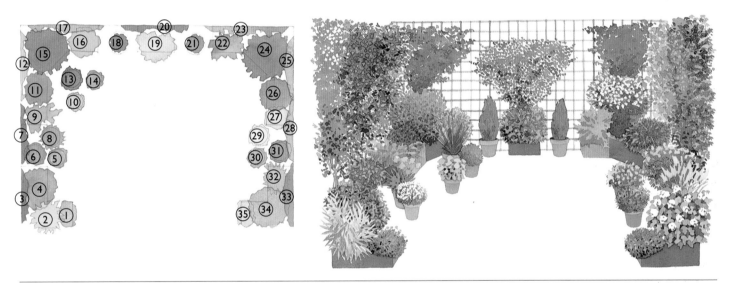

Designs for corners

A small group of pots can do wonders for a dull corner of a patio. Brought together in an artful arrangement, they will provide a burst of colour. The two groups shown here are intended for differing conditions: sun or shade. In either arrangement, the pots containing summer-flowering herbaceous perennials could be replaced with containers of spring bulbs to extend the interest.

Plants for semi shade

1 *Clematis macropetala*
2 *Vitis cognetiae*
3 *Hydrangea serrata* 'Preziosa'
4 *Acer palmatum dissectum atropurpureum*
5 *Agapanthus* Headbourne Hybrids
6 *Alchemilla mollis*
7 *Euonymus fortunei* 'Emerald 'n' Gold'

Sun or shade

Two imaginative plantings show how to liven up a 'dead' corner. Watering and feeding are essential for a healthy display.

Plants for sun

1 *Rosa* 'Alfred Carriere'
2 *Clematis* 'Elsa Spath'
3 *Elaeagnus* x *ebbingei* 'Limelight'
4 *Phormium tenax purpureum*
5 *Lilium regale*
6 *Ceanothus* 'Blue Mound'
7 *Sedum* 'Vera Jameson'
8 *Pinus* 'Hugo Ophir'

Problem areas

Apart from the main borders and beds that form the major elements of any garden planting, there are other areas where plants can add greatly to the atmosphere. They will enhance small corners and boundary walls, and special focal points, be they ponds, raised beds or alcoves. It is important to ensure that planting schemes in all parts of the garden are planned and considered in relation to each other. You can, of course, opt for several different themes, from a Mediterranean dry garden near a sunny patio to a shady, woodland garden under trees, but sudden, jarring transitions between one kind of planting and another need to be avoided. Colour is an important consideration, since an area of very strong colours – hot reds, yellows and vibrant purples – would make a pastel scheme look washed out in comparison if the two can be viewed simultaneously.

Creating a tranquil mood
A water feature blends in with the brick wall behind, allowing moisture-loving plants and climbers to grow together in a small space.

Disguising walls and fences

The vertical architecture of the garden – house walls, boundary walls and fences – provide a useful support for some plants and can be a great asset for the garden. Flowering climbers greatly increase the number of flowering plants you can cram into the smallest garden, and many will grow successfully in close proximity, so that roses and clematis, for example, can be intertwined, extending the flowering season and the colour value over a longer period. It pays to include some evergreen and foliage climbers so that the walls and fences are clothed in autumn and winter as well as summer. Climbing hydrangeas, ornamental vines and some of the creepers are ideal for this. Remember that some good climbers, like wisteria, are exceptionally vigorous – so be prepared to prune them regularly to contain them and encourage flowering.

Green wall
Pots of herbs sit on a ledge between a wall and fence that are camouflaged by ivy.

Awkward spots

In many gardens, there are odd corners that are difficult to deal with, often because they are heavily shaded. Any desire to plant a sun-loving perennial border on this kind of site is doomed to instant failure. However, a quieter, no-less effective planting solution can be achieved if you opt for foliage texture and colour instead of flower power.

Once you establish whether the area is dry or damp, you can select suitable shade-loving plants that will thrive in these conditions. Very dry shade will limit your choices, although ivies do well in this environment, and a few carefully chosen varieties, with a judiciously placed statue or handsome pot, can turn a dull, dark corner into one of mystery and excitement.

Hostas, ferns and even busy lizzies (impatiens) also cope very well with shade, while dicentra, tiarella and heuchera do well in semi-shade. Plants in pots are especially useful for these difficult corners. If necessary, you can occasionally move the containers into sunnier positions. In areas where nothing much will grow, use hard materials such as beach pebbles to create surface interest, and perhaps include a interesting ornament – a statue or a well-shaped piece of driftwood.

Secluded spot
Climbers adorn a high fence and trellis, obscuring the view of a nearby house and allowing space for shade-loving plants beneath.

Hiding eyesores

To hide an unattractive view within the garden or beyond its boundaries, you may want to provide a screen clothed in plants. You need to be careful, however, as although some plants will quickly mask the unwanted view, they may present problems of control at a later date.

Plants such as quick-growing elaeagnus with its silvery, evergreen leaves, will put on nearly as much growth per year as the notoriously fast-growing conifer, x *cupressocyparis leylandii*, but will stop at around 5m (15ft) – a much more useful proposition for a small garden.

Although the Russian vine (*Fallopia baldschuanica*) is often recommended as a quick screening plant, which it undoubtedly is, it is a real bruiser in its determination to swamp every plant (and structure) in the vicinity. Unless you are prepared to control it with equal vigour and determination, you would be wise to avoid it.

Trellis, against which a variety of twining climbers can be grown, makes an excellent screen for masking a work area or a vegetable plot, for example. As it allows the wind through rather than creating a barrier, you will not suffer from problems caused by wind tunnels.

Trellis is also a useful means of providing privacy and shelter around a sitting area. Equally useful for screening or shelter are large pots, in which shrubs can be grouped in different places at various times of the year, depending on your needs.

Under cover
A facade of trellis and plants is a good way to hide eyesores – from a work area to ugly drainpipes.

Large pots are best moved on a series of small metal rollers; do not try to move them otherwise, as they are extremely heavy.

Remember that almost any plant will survive in a pot, even a smallish tree,

providing it is well-watered during dry spells and fed throughout the growing season. Some plants to consider for this purpose are bamboos, yuccas, lilies, rhododendrons, box, yew and climbing roses.

Far corners

Many gardens have distant parts that are awaiting development. By planting naturally occurring species such as the humble nettle or cow parsley, you can turn such areas into wildlife havens, which will attract and bene-

Wildlife bonus
Naturally occurring flowers and grasses can turn a corner of the garden into a wildlife haven.

fit bees, butterflies and insects. Even in a much smaller garden you may still be able to find some space for a wildlife area, for instance by turning the end of a formal lawn into a wild-flower meadow.

This is also a useful labour-saving device in a large garden, as the grass will only need cutting twice a year, if native flowering plants and grasses are to be encouraged. A path can then be mown through the area, when the remainder of the grass is cut, to provide access. This looks very natural and appropriate.

In shadier, undeveloped corners, a tapestry of ground cover plants which require very little attention is the ideal solution. Your best bet is to choose plants that are naturally vigorous, but be prepared, once a year to remove any that are becoming too invasive.

Gravel corner
A gravel garden in a shady corner can be used to grow plants that like free-draining soil such as Centranthus *and some species of* Campanula.

CARE AND MAINTENANCE

For a garden to look its best, and the plants in it to flourish and grow, it must have the right care and attention. This means that to be successful, the gardener has to understand the garden's basic requirements, such as the best possible conditions in which to grow plants, when to supply water or feed, and how to keep them pest and disease-free. This section of the book is an invaluable point of reference for every novice gardener, explaining and illustrating exactly what needs to be done, and when, to keep the entire garden in optimum condition. From choosing the basic tools and equipment, through to learning about and improving the soil, controlling weeds, supporting, pruning and training trees, shrubs and plants, applying fertilizers and increasing your plant stocks, it provides a clear, comprehensive source of expert advice on every aspect of maintaining the garden. A must for all budding gardeners!

The natural environment

The aim of any gardener is to provide the optimum environment in which plants can grow and flourish, not only so that plants are healthy and strong but so that the garden as a whole looks well cared for and is used to its full potential. For successful gardening, it is essential to understand how the natural environment affects plant growth, and how plants respond to their growing conditions. To care for and maintain your garden, you need to organise your environment as efficiently as possible. This means knowing the basic requirements of plants, how climate affects growth, how to deal with soil, how to feed and water plants, and how to shape and control them. It is also useful to be able to increase your stock of plants, cheaply and easily, by growing them yourself from seeds or cuttings.

A border of healthy plants
A perennial border in full swing in summer is one of the great delights of gardening, but behind this seemingly artless mass of flowering plants lies a lot of hard work and hard-won experience.

Healthy plants

Plants need light, air, water and nourishment in order to flourish and thrive. A basic understanding of how plants grow and why each of these factors is important helps you to provide the best growing conditions for your plants. You also need to consider the local climate, as the temperature range, rainfall and wind will have a strong influence on the plants you choose, as well as where you position them and how you care for them afterwards.

How plants grow

Plants manufacture their own food by the process of photosynthesis. Sunlight is the prime energy source. All the green parts of a plant (not just the leaves) contain chlorophyll, which absorbs sunlight and converts it into energy. This energy then converts carbon dioxide from the atmosphere and water and nutrients from the soil into carbohydrates or food for the plant. The process of photosynthesis gives off

oxygen as a by-product. To ensure healthy growth, plants need some essential foods (nutrients). The most important of these are nitrogen (N), phosphorus (P) and potassium (K). Plants obtain these foods through their roots, by absorbing mineral salts from the soil. Each of these three nutrients contributes to the growth of the plant in different ways:
Nitrogen is vital for healthy leaf and stem growth.
Phosphorus promotes strong root growth.
Potassium is necessary for flowering and fruiting.
In fertile soils, these nutrients are naturally replenished in the never-ending cycle of plant death and decay. However, to get the best results from your plants, or to cure any nutritional deficiencies, it is often necessary to give extra nutrients in the form of fertilizers (see pp. 80–81).

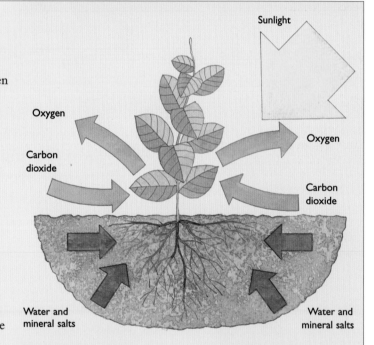

The growth cycle
An understanding of the way in which a plant obtains food makes it clear that light, air and water are essential for healthy growth. The diagram above shows how a plant uses sunlight, air and water to manufacture its food by the process known as photosynthesis. All parts of the plant are involved in this process. The delicate root hairs take up water and nutrients, in the form

of mineral salts, from the soil. Green leaves and stems contain chlorophyll which traps sunlight. Energy derived from sunlight is then used to convert the nutrients from the soil and carbon dioxide from the atmosphere into carbohydrate food for the plant. Oxygen, the gas essential to all life, is given off as a by-product. By growing plants, you contribute to the quality of the air we breathe.

Climate

Your gardening possibilities are affected by the climate in which you live, as are your gardening tasks.

Latitude, altitude and distance from the sea all determine local climate. Even in a small garden, it is possible to create some particular 'microclimate' to suit certain plants – a pond for moisture-loving plant types, or a sheltered, sunny spot for sun-lovers.

Temperature, rainfall and wind all play a part in the overall climate and each has a part in determining which plants grow well. In different parts of the world, plants have adapted to take advantage of the natural conditions. Water-retaining succulents and cacti survive in deserts, and plants with huge leaves grow successfully in the shade because they can expose the greatest possible area of leaf to the light and therefore manufacture food efficiently.

Gardening against the natural climate – trying to grow damp-loving plants in dry territory and vice versa – increases your workload enormously and produces disappointing results.

Temperature

The length of the growing season is governed by temperature, which also affects other aspects of plant growth. Air temperature often influences the rate of growth; for example, lawn grass starts to grow when temperatures rise above 6° C (43° F). Summer temperature determines whether or not many plants reach maturity and set seed. The chilling effect of winter, when plants are dormant, often determines the quality of flowers and seed germination in the following season.

Frost
Frost is a great danger to plants when the temperature consistently drops below freezing. Ice crystals form within the plant cells, causing them to split. Rapid thawing can then rupture cells. Symptoms of frost damage include blackened young shoots, shrivelled stems and leaves, and shoots, or even whole plants, that die back.

Frost lift squeezes young plants out of the soil as it freezes and thaws, exposing roots to drying wind and low temperatures. Wind chill (wind and low temperature) causes damage to plants.

Frost pockets
Because it is heavy, cold air runs downhill and frost collects at the lowest point to form a 'frost pocket'. When planting, ensure that you select specimens accordingly or plan to avoid these areas where plants are most vulnerable to damage.

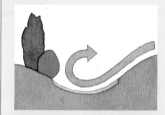

Frost collects in a valley
You can see here how cold air gathers over the frost pocket and extends the area of possible damage as it backs up the slope.

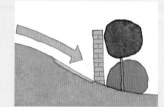

Frost in front of trees
A frost pocket will form in front of obstacles in the path of cold air. Removing them allows the cold air to pass through.

Rainfall

Any country with rainfall distributed evenly throughout the year provides ideal conditions for gardening, because rain and snow are the main sources of water for plants growing outdoors. Either too much or too little rain can be a problem.
Drought Much of the water provided by rainfall is lost through surface run-off and evaporation. Drought is a common problem, especially during summer. Wilting is the first sign of distress as the plant shuts down until more water is available. Plants that are native to dry areas often have specially adapted leaves, with a reduced surface area, to help reduce water loss.
Waterlogging Most plants are able to survive water-logging for short periods of time, but when it is prolonged, the roots are damaged and eventually die.

Rain shadow
In the lee of a house or other building, rain may scarcely penetrate the ground. Susceptible plants may suffer unless you ensure the soil stays moist. Grow plants in open ground, away from buildings and other structures, to get the full benefit from the rain.

Dry areas
The diagram shows that no rain falls on the side of a house facing away from the prevailing wind. Rain shadows also cause problems on the leeward sides of walls and solid fences.

Wind

Wind in the garden disperses seed and pollen, circulates air and discourages diseases. It can also create problems.
Windrock Affects young or recently transplanted plants. They rock to and fro causing root damage, slow growth or even death in dry conditions.
Windscorch May occur on very exposed sites. Plants lean away from the prevailing wind. Cold or dry winds make plant tops misshapen and kill growth buds.
Windthrow Causes the most extreme damage. Branches are torn away. During gales, whole trees may be lifted out of the ground.
Reduced growth The result of excessive water loss in high winds and in high temperatures. A plant's attempts to grow upright in strong winds can reduce its development by as much as 30 per cent.

Wind protection
Windbreaks provide shelter, often crucial for young or recently transplanted plants. Fences, screens and hedges all filter the wind whereas a solid windbreak may create more turbulence. Tie young trees to stakes to protect them.

Hedge windbreak
A hedge provides good shelter from cold winds and allows an early-season display of container-grown tulips and other spring flowers.

Basic equipment

Providing the best care for your plants, and keeping the garden looking good all year round, requires regular maintenance. To do this easily and efficiently, you need a range of gardening tools and equipment. Such tools are often expensive. For the new gardener faced with a vast array of differing shapes and brands, deciding what to buy may present a daunting task. However, with careful planning it can be easier than you think.

First, think about the type of garden you would like. It could be one that takes little maintenance for example, or one with no lawn. Or it could be devoted exclusively to growing vegetables. The style of garden will entirely influence the choice of tools. If you have a lawn, you will need mowing equipment; if you grow vegetables, you will need tools for cultivation.

Invest in the best-quality items you can afford and do not be tempted to economize. If necessary, buy just a few well-made tools for essential tasks, as they will be more comfortable to use, will last longer and do a better job.

Safety is an important consideration in gardening (see p. 73). Your eyes are particularly vulnerable, so it is important to wear goggles if you are using cutting equipment. Always remember to cover up the sharp points of canes and poles, for further protection.

Digging and cultivating tools

These tools are the most frequently used in the garden and it is worth buying the best you can afford.

Forks and spades
A good spade and fork are vital. Use the spade for digging and breaking up the ground and lifting soil. Use the fork for general cultivation, lifting plants and forking manure and compost.

Before you buy a fork or spade, handle it to get an idea of the weight and balance, looking for strength combined with lightness. Check that the joint between the shaft and the head is secure and that all surfaces, especially the handles, are smooth to avoid blisters. Handles are shaped in the form of a T, D, or YD. Try all three to find which design you find more comfortable to use. A smooth surface on the blades or tines makes working with, and cleaning tools much easier.

Spades and forks come in three basic sizes: **digging** (the largest); **medium**; and **border**, (the smallest). Choose the size which feels most comfortable for you.

A Cornish shovel, similar to a spade, has a longer handle and is useful if more leverage is needed.

Hoes
Use these for cultivating the topsoil and weeding around plants. There are two main types:
Push or 'Dutch' hoe Cuts through surface weeds with a slicing action.
Draw hoe (Also called a swan-neck hoe). Used with a chopping action for weeding. Also for making lines or drills for seeds.

Rakes
Use rakes for breaking up the soil and levelling it before planting. The greater the number of teeth in the rake, the finer the soil surface.

Trowels and hand forks
These, too, are essential. Use a trowel for digging holes and planting. They are also handy for working in containers and raised beds. Use a hand fork for weeding, lifting small plants and for planting. Hand forks are available with round or flat tines. The flat-tined type is better for weeding.

Mechanical digger
For digging large areas a motorized Rotovator can be hired, but do not use them on soils with many perennial weeds as they create ideal conditions for their regrowth by dispersing the stems.

Trowel

Hand fork (round tines)

Hand fork (flat tines)

Spade

Draw hoe

Dutch hoe

Rake

Fork

Cornish shovel

Basic digging and cultivating equipment
These tools will be in use all the time as you care for your garden. Good-quality tools last longer and are more comfortable to work with.

Cutting and pruning tools

Many garden maintenance tasks involve restricting or shaping plant growth. Good training and pruning of plants gives the garden an attractive form, as well as keeping the plants healthy. The kind of cutting and pruning tools you need depends on the planting style of your garden. All cutting tools should be kept clean, sharp and in good condition, ready for use.

Knives

Perhaps the most useful tool is a really good-quality, sharp knife. Most gardeners carry one in their pocket (the kind that closes up safely is imperative). The knife should be well-balanced, strong, light and comfortable to use.

Gardening knife Used for dead-heading plants, harvesting fruit and vegetables, and taking cuttings, as well as cutting string or canes.

Pruning knife Has a curved blade for controlled pruning.

Secateurs

Heavy-duty cutting – of slender wooden stems and branches – demands a pair of secateurs. These have two blades which meet in a chopping action as the handles are squeezed. Be careful not to pinch your fingers when pressing the secateur handles together. Left- or right-handed models are available, and there are three main types:

Anvil With a single, straight-edged cutting blade that closes down on to an anvil (a bar of softer metal, often brass). A **ratchet** modification enables the user to cut through a branch in stages which makes pruning less tiring and is ideal for those with a small handspan.

Manaresi Has two blades, both with straight cutting edges. These are often used for pruning vines.

Bypass The best all-purpose secateurs. They have a convex upper blade that cuts against a concave lower one.

When using secateurs, position the stem to be cut close to the base of the blade where it can be held firmly. If the cut is made with the tip, the blades are liable to be strained or forced apart.

Shears

Shears have a similar action to secateurs but longer, flatter blades. There is usually a notch at the base of one blade for cutting tough stems, but thick stems will need pruners or a saw. Use shears to clip hedges or topiary, cut back herbaceous plants and areas of long grass. They should be strong, light, sharp and comfortable to use.

Loppers and saws

These are used for stouter branches.

General-purpose pruning saw Copes with most pruning needs.

Folding pruning saw The blade closes into the handle (like a pen-knife). Handy for most tasks except sawing through large branches.

Bow saw Good for tougher branches.

Long-handled pruners or loppers Strong secateurs with long handles to give extra leverage when cutting thick stems or branches.

Cutting and pruning tools

Using the right cutting tool for the job is essential if you are to avoid blunting tools and damaging plants by bruising and ragged cuts.

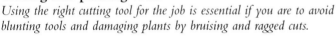

Garden knife

Anvil secateurs

Manaresi secateurs

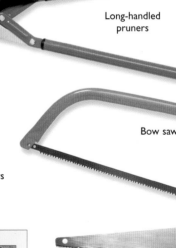
Long-handled pruners

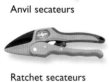
Pruning knife

Ratchet secateurs

Bypass secateurs

Bow saw

General purpose pruning saw

Folding pruning saw

Shears

Tool care

Tools will not last or function well if they are dirty, rusty or damaged. Clean all tools immediately after use, and wipe metal surfaces with an oily rag.

Mechanized equipment should be regularly oiled. Wipe electrically powered tools dry and clean before they are stored.

It is important to sharpen cutting tools on a regular basis as blunt blades will damage the plants.

Sharpening knives
Hold the knife blade at a 25° angle and push it gently along a moistened oilstone. Repeat this process on both sides of the blade until the knife is sharp.

Lawn care equipment

The kind of lawn you want will determine the lawn tools you need. A formal lawn, complete with stripes of mown grass and neatly cut edges, will require a cylinder mower (see p. 90) and an edging iron and shears. A wild meadow-style lawn will only need to be cut once or twice a year with a sickle or scythe (see p. 91), or an electric strimmer.

The lawn hand tools are illustrated below right. The power tools you need will depend on the size and form of your garden. You would be well advised to discuss your precise requirements with a reputable garden centre.

Other useful tools are:
Sickle Has a very sharp curved blade mounted on a wooden or plastic handle. Useful for trimming areas of long grass. It must be kept sharp.
Fan rake A wire rake used to remove moss and to aerate the lawn.

Lawn tools

There are two vital tools for well-defined lawn edges.
Long-handled edging shears Used to trim any long grass straggling from the lawn edges. Use these every 14 days when the grass is growing vigorously.
Edging iron Use three or four times during the growing season to cut away long grass or rough edges.

Lawn maintenance tools
Such tools will achieve a neat lawn with sharp edges, helping to make a garden appear well tended.

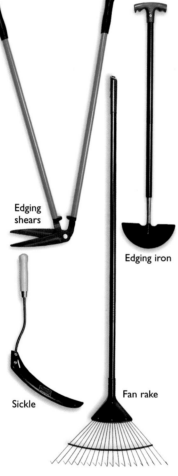

Edging shears

Edging iron

Sickle

Fan rake

Lawnmowers
Choose the lawnmower which best suits your lawn.
Manual lawnmowers Adequate for a small lawn, these are quiet and need little maintenance.
Power lawnmowers Run off petrol or electricity and have one of two cutting actions – cylinder or rotary. For an even, top quality lawn the cylinder type is the best.

Rotary and hover mowers are good for uneven ground but do cut less closely. Rotary mowers have wheels, hover types glide on a cushion of air. For a striped effect, make sure your mower has a fitted roller.

Electric hover mower
This hover mower is good for small areas of lawn. It cuts quickly but not very closely.

Spraying equipment

You may need to spray your plants, either to apply weedkillers or pesticides, or just to mist the leaves with water or give a foliar feed.

Sprayers range from simple, hand-held types, operated by pressing a lever at the top, through to pressurized devices with a pump mechanism. The higher the operating pressure, the greater the risk of harmful chemicals in weedkillers or pesticides drifting onto surrounding plants and harmless insects. Always use on windless days and wear protective clothing, as directed by the manufacturer of the spray and wash sprayers out thoroughly after use.

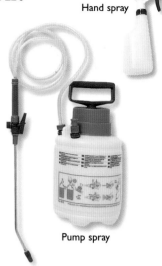

Hand spray

Pump spray

Basic sprayers
Choose from a range of simple hand-held sprayers through to pressurized devices for larger areas.

Carrying equipment

You will often need to move materials within the garden. For instance, you may want to shift soil from one area to another, clear away prunings or move flower pots.

Wheelbarrows

These are essential for moving heavy or loose materials over short distances. Choose a well-balanced model. When the barrow is full, the bulk of the weight should rest over the wheel and not towards the handles. This will make it easier to manoeuvre.

Wheelbarrow

Bags, ground sheets and waste sacks

These are perfect for collecting and carrying light, bulky items such as grass or hedge clippings. They can be folded flat for storage. Woven mesh plastic is the ideal material as it is durable and less likely to rip or tear. Broad, flat handle straps make carrying heavy weights easier.

Trug baskets and buckets

These are ideal for light work such as harvesting flowers and vegetables, or collecting and transporting a few weeds. There are both plastic and traditional wooden types available in a range of sizes.

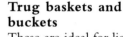

Carry bag

Trug

Watering equipment

Seedlings, newly transplanted plants and those grown in containers all need regular watering for healthy growth. Some kind of watering equipment is necessary, although a simple watering can may be all you need.

Watering cans

A good-quality can is a must. Choose a well-balanced one that starts to pour as soon as it is tilted, with a long spout for extra reach. Watering cans range from 0.5 to 15 litres (16 fl oz to 3 gallons). A rose (nozzle) can be fitted to give an even spray.

Hosepipes and fittings

You will need a hosepipe for watering distant parts of the garden or for heavy watering. Most are made of PVC, but vary in quality and price.
Lances and pistols Fit these to the end of a hose to give a fine jet of water or as extensions for reaching inaccessible plant containers.

Sprinklers

These are useful for an even watering of quite large areas.
Oscillating Gives an even spray over a rectangular area.
Rotary Gives even coverage over a circular area.
Static Sprays water in a circle. This is the best type of sprinkler for lawns.

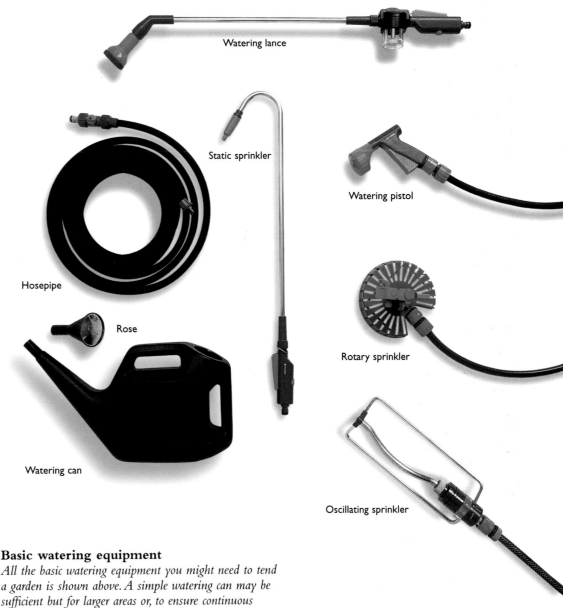

Watering lance

Static sprinkler

Watering pistol

Hosepipe

Rose

Rotary sprinkler

Watering can

Oscillating sprinkler

Basic watering equipment
All the basic watering equipment you might need to tend a garden is shown above. A simple watering can may be sufficient but for larger areas or, to ensure continuous watering, a hose or sprinkler will make life much easier.

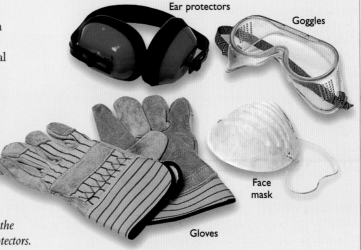

Garden safety

Whenever you are using garden machinery or equipment, always play safe by wearing the appropriate protective clothing.

If you are in any doubt about what to wear, look on the machine itself, for safety symbols that show you the minimum you should wear for safe use.

Most accidents occur while mowers, hedge trimmers,.spades, forks and secateurs are being used. Do wear strong boots and always have electrical tools fitted with a residual current device (RCD) to cut out the electrical circuit. Do not use electrical tools in damp weather.

Basic safety equipment
Tough gardening gloves are essential for the keen gardener. Protect your eyes with goggles when using power tools or cutting implements. For dusty or dirty jobs, wear a face mask. Cut out the noise of power tools with ear protectors.

Ear protectors

Goggles

Face mask

Gloves

Knowing your soil

The most important resource in any garden is the soil in which the plants grow. Most soil is capable of supporting plant life but by cultivating your soil well, you greatly increase the health and beauty of your plants. Fertile soil is well-drained and aerated, and is rich in organic matter. It is also full of invisible but highly beneficial micro-organisms and bacteria. Digging properly, improving drainage and adding plenty of organic matter and some fertilizer will improve soil texture and structure and the activity of helpful bacteria.

Soil types

Soils are classified according to the proportions of sand, silt or clay. These three materials have quite different properties which determine the character of the soil.
Sandy soils have little or no clay in them, which makes them very light and free-draining. Nutrients are quickly washed away and the soil can dry out. They are easy to work and quick to warm up in spring.
Silty soils are more fertile and retain water better than sandy soils. They can be difficult to work, though, and often form a surface crust or cap. This can be a problem because rainwater runs off and fertilizers are not taken up very easily.

Clay soils are usually rich in nutrients and retain water well, but they tend to take time to warm up in spring and are slow to drain. They are prone to compaction and can be difficult to work. In hot, dry summers, clays are liable to bake and crack.
The ideal is **loam**, a mixture of sand, silt and clay. It has many of the better characteristics of all three, such as high fertility, good water-holding qualities and good drainage.

As well as these main soil types, there is organic soil. Peat, as it is usually called, consists of thick layers of decomposed organic matter (such as leaves, grasses and moss). Peat soils often have poor drainage and lack useful nutrients.

How to improve your soil

Soil type	Problems	Treatment
Sandy	Light and very free draining; loses nutrients quickly	Add humus (p. 78) and fertilizers (p. 80)
Silty	Soil particles are very tightly packed so surface compacts easily; especially sticky to work	Dig over to open up structure (p. 84), then add humus (p. 78) and fertilizers (p. 80)
Clay	Soil is slow to drain, heavy and difficult to work; surface cracks in dry weather	Improve drainage (p. 76); dig thoroughly (p. 84); add lime (p. 81) and humus (p. 78)
Loam	None	Add humus (p. 78) and fertilizers (p. 80)
Peat	Slow to drain and very acid; lacks nutrients unless drained and limed	Improve drainage (p. 76) and add lime (p. 81)

Plants for sandy and clay soils

Once you have ascertained what type of soil you have, you will need to choose plants that suit these conditions. Certain plants, including those listed below, prefer a light, free-draining soil and will do particularly well on sandy soils, although you may have to add well-rotted compost or manure to improve moisture retention. Clay soils can be heavy and difficult to work but there are many plants that will grow well in this type of soil. Despite its problems, it is full of much-needed nutrients and holds water well, making it ideal for the plants listed.

Plants for sandy soil

Trees	Shrubs	Perennials
Cercis siliquastrum	Brachyglottis	Agapanthus
Crataegus	Calluna	Alchemilla
Gleditsia	Cistus	Anthemis
Laburnum	Coronilla	Centranthus
	Cytisus	Echinops
	Eucalyptus	Eryngium
	Fuchsia	Kniphofia
	Gaultheria	Lupinus
	Genista	Lychnis
	Hebe	Monarda
	Helianthemum	Papaver
	Lonicera	Scabiosa
	Potentilla	Verbascum

Gleditsia
triacanthos

Plants for clay soil

Trees	Shrubs	Perennials
Fraxinus	Aronia	Bergenia
Laburnum	Aucuba	Campanula
Malus	Buddleja	Delphinium
Populus	Chaenomeles	Geranium
	Corylus	Gypsophila
	Escallonia	Helenium
	Euonymus	Hemerocallis
	Ligustrum	Ligularia
	Mahonia	Persicaria
	Philadelphus	Phlox
	Pyracantha	Ranunculus
	Ribes	Rudbeckia
	Spiraea	Solidago
	Viburnum	Thalictrum

Helenium
'Gartensonne'

The chemical balance

The degree of acidity or alkalinity (the pH) of the soil affects the type of plants that you can grow. Although most plants will grow in soil with a wide range of pH values, certain plants have specific requirements. If your soil is extremely acidic or alkaline, you will have problems and it may be necessary to make some effort to alter the natural balance.

You can easily test your soil to check its natural acid/alkaline balance using a soil-testing kit (see right). The pH level can vary significantly within a given plot, so when testing take samples from different areas within the garden.

Soil pH
Soil acidity and alkalinity are measured on a scale of pH ranging from 0 to 14. A pH below 7 indicates acid soil, and above 7 is alkaline. A pH of 7 is neutral. Between 5.5 and 7.5 suits most plants.

Maintaining soil pH
Cultivated ground tends to become more acidic, which can be corrected by adding lime. Make sure that it is necessary, as applying too much can be harmful. Follow the instructions given for quantities for different soil types. Do not apply lime and manure together because the nutritional value of manure is depleted by chemical reaction.

Growing mediums
If you happen to have alkaline soil, and a particular desire to grow acid-loving plants such as rhododendrons, camellias or heathers, the best way to do this is to grow them in containers using a specially formulated growing medium.

This growing mix would be impractical and much too expensive to use over a large area, but it does allow you to grow a few favourite specimens either in individual containers or in a raised bed. These specially formulated mixes for acid-loving plants are often labelled 'ericaceous' (for heathers) or rhododendron mixes, and are usually based on peat rather than soil.

Bear in mind, however, that if your tapwater contains lime, you may need to use an acid fertilizer from time to time in order to correct the soil balance (see p. 80).

Testing the pH of your soil

Simple pH testing kits are widely available in garden centres. They are very easy to use and enable you to pinpoint exactly where your soil lies in the pH range.

Read the results of your testing against the card provided with the soil-testing kit for an accurate indication of pH. When testing your soil take samples from various areas of the garden because the pH level can vary. If you have a new garden to cultivate it is a good idea to test the soil before you buy any plants.

1 *Using a pipette, put some of the soil solution in the smaller compartment of a soil-testing kit. Shake the solution and let it settle.*

2 *Using the colour chart provided with the testing kit check the colour of the solution to determine the pH level of your soil.*

Sample pH readings

Acid soil
If testing results in a yellow or orange colour it indicates an acid soil.

Neutral soil
If testing results in a pale green colour it reveals that the soil is neutral.

Alkaline soil
If testing results in a dark green/blue colour it shows that the soil is alkaline.

Plants for acid or alkaline soils

Most plants are not fussy about pH values and grow well in a wide range of soils. There are exceptions: rhododendrons and many heathers, for example, only flourish in acid soils. Before buying plants check whether your soil is acid or alkaline and which plants grow best in such soil. Although it is possible, in a minor way to adjust the balance by adding lime or peat, major changes are out of the question and you will always get the healthiest plants by buying those that suit your conditions. It is very difficult to grow lime-loving plants on acid soil and almost impossible to grow lime-hating plants on alkaline soil. However, you can grow both types of plants in containers or raised beds. A selection of the most popular acid-loving and alkali-loving plants is listed below.

***Pieris* 'Forest Flame'**

Plants for acid soil
Acer palmatum
Camellia japonica
Cercidiphyllum japonicum
Cornus kousa
Epimedium grandiflorum
Kalmia latifolia
Liquidambar styraciflua
Pieris japonica
Rhododendron

Brunnera macrophylla

Plants for alkaline soil
Anchusa azurea
Aquilegia vulgaris
Brunnera macrophylla
Kolkwitzia amabalis
Lonicera periclymenum
Morus nigra
Phlomis fruticosa
Syringa microphylla
Verbascum phoeniceum

Drainage

Well-drained soil allows a good supply of air and water to reach the roots of plants. As a result strong, healthy roots are developed that can extract water at a lower depth in the soil, helping plants to survive in dry conditions. In well-drained soil, too, the sun can warm the ground more quickly, making it possible to plant and sow earlier in the year.

On badly drained soil, root growth is restricted and plants develop shallow root systems that are unable to reach water in a drought. In wet weather the ground becomes waterlogged and roots die through lack of air.

Alpine plants
A gravel mulch improves drainage and retains heat well. It is ideal around alpine plants which need a free-draining environment.

Draining the ground

If the drainage problem is not too serious, adding generous quantities of organic matter, such as well-rotted compost, straw or leaf mould improves the texture of the soil and aids drainage. On very heavy, clay soils, digging in large amounts of coarse grit also helps drainage.

If the drainage problem is one of surface water, slope the soil to produce a slight fall, allowing water to run away into drains or ditches. Another option is to grow crops in raised beds or ridges to keep the roots drier. The water can be channelled away in the bottom of the ridge.

If the water table is too close to the surface you may have to install a system of drainpipes, probably with the help of a specialist contractor. Perforated plastic pipes or tile drains are usually arranged in a herringbone pattern, on a layer of gravel, in trenches about 60–75cm (24–30in) deep. Slope the trenches gently towards the lowest point in the garden. On sloping ground lay the pipes parallel to the surface. Place a layer of ash or gravel over the pipes before filling the trench, to intercept the water in the soil and direct it towards the pipes. If there is no natural outlet, such as a ditch or stream, it may be necessary to construct a soakaway (a gravel-filled pit).

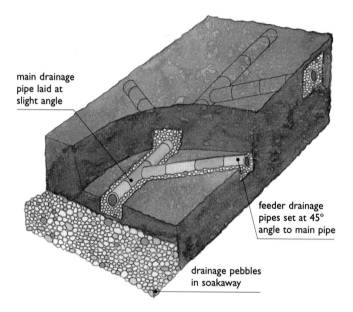

main drainage pipe laid at slight angle

feeder drainage pipes set at 45° angle to main pipe

drainage pebbles in soakaway

Simple drainage system
A herringbone pattern of drainpipes laid in gravel-filled trenches carries away excess water. The branch drains feed into the main drain which carries away the water to an outlet or a soakaway pit.

Testing for drainage
Installing a drainage system is hard work and can be very expensive, so it is well worth testing the soil first to gauge the extent of the problem.

The best and easiest test to carry out is to dig a hole about 60cm (24in) deep. Leave the hole exposed until after a period of heavy rain and then observe how high the water level within the hole rises and, in particular, how long it takes for the rainwater to drain away again. The chart (right) will help you to determine whether any action needs to be taken and recommends the best way to improve the drainage in your garden.

Another simple way of detecting bad drainage is to look closely at the colour of the soil in the hole, particularly in the lower levels. If the soil is a bluish-grey colour with small rusty-brown marks this is a sure sign of very poor drainage.

Drainage	Signs	Action
Good	No water in hole a few days after rain	None
Poor	Some water at bottom of hole a few days after rain	Double dig and add organic material
Excessive	No water in hole 1 hour after rain	Add humus
Impeded	Hole still partly full a few days after rain	Dig in organic material and/or install drains

Mulches

A significant amount of moisture is lost by water evaporating from the soil surface into the atmosphere. This can be a major problem for shallow-rooted plants. Covering the soil with a suitable material – a mulch – drastically reduces moisture loss and will also suppress weeds that compete with your garden plants for water. The open texture of some mulching materials can help to improve surface drainage as well. Always apply the mulch to damp soil, otherwise you reduce the amount of rain reaching the soil. A good time to mulch is after the spring rain when the ground has warmed up.

Inorganic mulches

These mulches (especially plastic sheeting) are extremely effective for conserving moisture.

This continuous 'blanket' over the soil acts as a barrier and also blocks out the light, which prevents weed seeds from germinating. The main disadvantage of such mulches is that they look rather unattractive. To improve the appearance, disguise sheeting by covering it with a shallow layer (2–3cm, or 1in) of composted bark or shingle.

By protecting sheeting from the sun in this way you will also help to extend its working life.

Fibre fleece
A lightweight mulch that raises soil temperatures.

Woven black plastic
Good between vegetable rows Expensive, but re-usable.

Plants in inorganic mulch
Plants benefit from soil-moisture retention and weed supression but gain nothing of nutrional value.

Black plastic
A cheap mulch that is effective at killing weeds and slightly raising the temperature of the soil.

Grit
Useful for plants which need free drainage. Plants self-seed in it if it is not used over plastic sheets.

Pebbles
Useful for absorbing the ambient heat and conserving soil moisture.

Organic mulches

To be totally effective, mulches should be 10cm (4in) thick to form a complete ground cover. Some of these mulches, such as coarsely shredded bark and leaf mould, will help to improve surface drainage.

Over a period of time some organic mulches will gradually improve the fertility of the soil as they decompose and become incorporated into its upper layers. The soil environment around the roots will also improve as this organic layer will encourage the activity of bacteria and worms.

Unfortunately the mulch may get scattered from time to time as birds forage for the worms. The heavier the mulch type, the less likely it is to become scattered by birds or wind.

Wood chippings
An effective weed suppressor. With a small electric chipper you can shred your own prunings.

Farmyard manure
Very valuable for enriching the fertility of the soil, it should only be used when it is well-rotted.

Plants in organic mulch
As well as moisture retention and weed suppression, benefits include added nutrients and worm activity.

Cacao fibre
This is fairly slow to break down, as well as expensive, so reserve it for use on your flower borders.

Coarse bark
Larger pieces of bark are longer lasting but expensive. Use them in ornamental borders.

Leaf mould
Good for protecting plants in winter and improving soil drainage. Needs topping up.

Improving your soil

Humus is essential to healthy soil, helping it to sustain plant growth. It consists of well-decayed organic matter, rich in beneficial micro-organisms. By adding humus on a regular basis, you improve drainage of heavy soils and increase the water retention of lighter ones. It promotes air flow through the soil, by improving texture, and as well as feeding plants, it stimulates beneficial bacteria and micro-organisms. These break down the nutrients in the soil to make them more accessible to plants. The end result of regular applications of humus is a more workable and more fertile soil. Humus is a term which is also used to describe partially decomposed, organic matter, such as peat, leaf mould and well-rotted farmyard manure. Producing your own compost from household waste and making leaf mould are both easy ways to provide yourself with ready supplies of humus.

Compost

A compost heap is an inexpensive way of recycling your domestic and garden waste. A properly tended heap accelerates the rotting down of organic matter into valuable, humus-rich compost. Regular applications over the years will make a substantial difference by enriching and improving the structure of all types of soil. Good compost is a rich, dark brown colour and has a light crumbly texture.

For successful compost, do not take large amounts of one specific material, but use each material in small amounts and alternate them in thin layers. Maintain a good supply of air and moisture. Materials decompose more quickly in spring and summer than in autumn or winter.

In summer, compost can be produced in just two to three months, but it could take at least three or four months during winter. You can build your own compost bin or buy one ready-made. If you have space, it is well worth having two bins so that while one heap is decomposing, the already rotted material can be dug in or spread around the garden soil.

Compost heaps

It is best to build a compost heap on level soil, rather than on an impermeable surface such as concrete, so that any rainwater or liquid from the decomposition process drains away freely. Choose a shady, sheltered site to avoid the drying effect of sun and wind.

The bottom layer or 'bed' of the compost heap should consist of a fibrous material such as straw or green hedge clippings, scattered loosely to allow a good flow of air.

Build up the heap in alternating layers of waste materials, ensuring that no single layer of material is too deep and that air can circulate freely. Alternate layers of carbon-rich material, woody fibrous stuff such as wood shavings or bark, about 10cm (4in) deep, with nitrogen-rich layers of green material like annual weeds or cabbage leaves about 20cm (8in) deep. (See opposite for compost materials). No layer should be solidly packed. Varying fast and slow-rotting materials in this way provides the most rapid rate of decomposition.

A compost primer can be used to accelerate the start of the rotting process. There are several proprietary compost primers, but cheap nitrogenous fertilizers, such as sulphate of ammonia, are just as effective. Adding manure or soil to every third layer of material obtains the best results as these natural additives are plentiful in the bacteria that are essential for breaking down waste.

Keep the heap moist if the weather is dry, adding water when necessary. Keep the top covered with a piece of plastic or old carpet to help retain moisture and reduce the heat loss. Turn the heap after two or three weeks, moving the sides to the middle. This will introduce a fresh supply of air to stimulate bacteria and ensure that the material in the heap composts evenly.

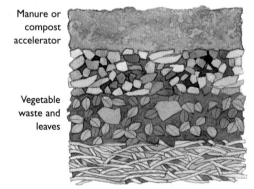

Manure or compost accelerator

Finely shredded prunings

Vegetable waste and leaves

Straw and hedge clippings

Layering compost
Alternate nitrogen-rich material, which decays quickly, with layers of carbon-rich waste, which decomposes slowly. Add compost primer to accelerate the rotting process.

Compost bins
A wide range of containers in different shapes and sizes and constructed from various materials can be bought ready-made. It is relatively easy, however, to make your own bin.

The most important factor is to ensure that the bin has a good air flow to promote rapid decomposition of the contents. The main purpose of the bin walls is to hold the composting material in place and keep it tidy. But the bonus of a container is that the compost remains moist at its edges rather than drying out.

For small gardens, a purpose-built compost bin is not necessary; black plastic sacks with holes made in the sides provide a satisfactory environment for composting leaves and garden waste.

Compost covers
Cover compost to conserve essential heat and to stop it from drying out. The plastic bin comes with its own lid while the wooden bins use a layer of carpet and a sheet of clear plastic.

Mulched border
Plants, such as hostas (left), that prefer rich, moist soil will greatly benefit from well-mulched soil, which helps to retain moisture while also adding nutrients.

Healthy harvest
Adding home-made compost to the soil on a regular basis is a cheap way of ensuring a supply of healthy herbs and vegetables from a fertile, productive soil.

Compost materials

Most vegetable material from the garden and kitchen will rot down and be suitable for making compost, provided it is not contaminated with chemicals or diseased.

Suitable materials
✓ Soft pruning and hedge clippings.
✓ Fallen leaves or flowers.
✓ Annual weeds, but not those that are seeding.
✓ Straw and sawdust.
✓ Torn newspapers and egg boxes, soaked in water.
✓ Vegetables and household waste; peelings, tea leaves, coffee grounds, egg shells etc.

Unsuitable materials
✗ Animal remains; encourages scavengers such as mice, rats and foxes.
✗ Cooked and greasy food; also encourages scavengers.
✗ Grass clippings; unless they are added in thin layers. Never use clippings from the first cut after applying selective 'hormone' weedkillers. These are very persistent chemicals, which may harm plants up to two years after they are used
✗ Woody material; unless it has first been thoroughly shredded.
✗ Badly diseased plants, such as potatoes infected with eelworm or cabbages suffering from clubroot.
✗ Perennial weeds that are flowering or any perennial weed roots.

Shredder
A shredder is very useful for chopping prunings into compostable material.

Leaf mould

This material is an excellent source of humus and a valuable soil conditioner. Decaying leaves contain relatively low levels of nutrients and are essentially a source of bulky, organic matter. Dig decayed leaf mould into the soil, or use it as a mulch. Beech and oak leaves decompose faster than other deciduous leaves and provide a generally acid compost, ideal for mulching acid-loving plants, such as rhododendrons and camellias.

Gathering leaves
Autumn leaves are a valuable source of bulky organic matter. Rake them up and stack them in a wire net cage or in a perforated black plastic bag. Use them to condition the soil a year later.

Plant foods

To grow well, plants need a balanced diet of nutrients. Nitrogen, phosphorous and potassium are the foods plants must have in large amounts to sustain a good growth rate. Nitrogen is needed for healthy growth and leaves, phosphorus is essential for good root development and potassium ensures both healthy flowers and fruits, and disease resistance.

As a gardener, you should supply your plants with these nutrients in various forms depending on the circumstances. Some forms are particularly useful for conditioning the soil, others for supplying a direct source of food to the plant itself. Quantities of nutrients required depend on how intensively the garden is cultivated: closely packed vegetables require a great deal; shrub borders much less. Fertilizers contain plant nutrients in a concentrated form and are used in fairly small quantities. Manures are bulky and need to be added to the soil in large amounts – but they provide only a small quantity of nutrients. However, they do add valuable fibre, which is converted into humus to condition the soil. This also increases the activity of beneficial micro-organisms.

Fertilizers

These may be organic or inorganic in their origin. **Organic fertilizers** consist of dead plant or animal matter that has been processed, such as bonemeal, dried blood and fishmeal. They do not scorch foliage and are natural products. **Inorganic fertilizers**, also known as artificial, chemical or synthetic fertilizers, are derived from mineral deposits or manufactured by an industrial process. These are highly concentrated and faster-acting than organic types, but do not exceed the dosage, or plants may be scorched or damaged. Fertilizers can be applied in dried form or dissolved in water, as in liquid feed.

Soil conditioners

Digging in quantities of bulky, organic matter introduces both nutrients and fibre into a garden soil. Green vegetation and manures with animal content provide some nutrients almost immediately, but very little fibre.

Woody and fibrous material is much better for opening heavy soils and improving the soil structure. It provides materials that improve moisture retention on lighter soils. Fibrous conditioners of this kind are ideal if long-term soil improvement is the ultimate aim. When they decompose they contribute to the formation of humus which absorbs other nutrients applied to the soil, apart from home-made garden compost and the different types of animal manures. Lime, while not a food, is also used to condition the soil. Never apply lime to the soil at the same time as fertilizers and manures.

Green manure
Organic matter can be added to the soil by growing a fast-maturing crop as temporary ground cover, on a bed that is empty for a while, usually over the winter. The crop is dug into the top soil six to eight weeks after germinating. This fast-maturing crop is known as a green manure and it is a means of improving both organic matter and nitrogen levels. The release of nitrogen is quite swift and so provides an early boost to plant growth. The greener and younger the manure, the less fibre is produced. Green manure crops should not be allowed time to flower or to set seed.

A green manure returns more to the ground than it has taken out, and eventually forms humus within the soil. Green plants with a rapid growth rate that mature quickly are the most popular green manure crops. Legumes are especially valuable, as they are able to fix atmospheric nitrogen.

Plants that are worth sowing include, for example, borage, comfrey, mustard, red clover and ryegrass.

1 *Mustard* (Sinapis alba) *is a useful green manure. Cut down the crop just before it flowers and leave cuttings on the surface to rot down.*

2 *Incorporate the cut foliage into the top few centimetres of soil with a spade or cultivator. The green leaf will decompose rapidly, thus improving soil fertility.*

Composting animal manure
Animal manure is one of the best soil conditioners because it improves soil texture and provides some nutrients while the straw provides bulk. Compost manure for at least six months, preferably for up to a year.

Dry fertilizers

These are nutrients in a dry, solid form – granules and pellets. They are mixed together and coated with a wax or resin compound which slowly dissolves and releases fertilizers into the soil. The release can take from six to 18 months, depending on the thickness of the outer coating, soil moisture, temperature and pH. Apply these fertilizers by sprinkling them evenly over the soil and mixing them into the top layer with a fork. If the soil is dry, water the area after application to dissolve the fertilizer and wash it down to the root zone. An even distribution is essential as damage to plants may occur if too much is used. Mark out the area into squares with canes and garden lines, as shown.

Liquid fertilizers

Liquid is usually easier and safer to apply than dry fertilizer, and the plant's response is often more rapid. The concentrated fertilizer can be bought either as liquid or powder which is diluted in water. It is applied either to the soil or to the leaves, depending on the type. Mix the fertilizer thoroughly with the water before application, to reduce the chance of damaging the plants. Do not apply when rain is forecast or it may be washed through the soil away from the plant's roots.

Nutrients applied to leaves as a foliar feed work rapidly and can be directed to specific areas. This is useful for plants with damaged roots, or if the soil is very dry. Apply foliar feed early in the day or when cloudy to avoid sun scorching the sprayed leaves.

Applying lawn fertilizer
Because fertilizers are heavily concentrated it is important to apply exactly the measured amount to a marked out area.

Applying plant fertilizer
Always apply fertilizer evenly, following the instructions given. Avoid touching the foliage as fertilizer can scorch plant leaves.

1 *Dilute liquid fertilizers with water and apply with a watering can or a hosepipe. These fast-acting feeds are useful for correcting nutritional deficiencies.*

2 *Apply liquid fertilizers as a foliar feed, or directly to the soil around the base of a plant. Most foliar feeds are soil-acting so any run-off is absorbed by the roots.*

Feeding container-grown plants

To promote balanced and healthy growth, use proprietary composts that contain measured amounts of fertilizer.

Additional feeds can be given if necessary by applying quick-acting fertilizers as a top dressing, or by using foliar feed or fertilizer spikes.

Fertilizer spikes
These spikes release their nutrients gradually into the compost. Insert them according to manufacturers' instructions.

Applying fertilizers

Type	Purpose and speed of absorption	How and when to apply	How much
Bulky organic matter (manure and compost)	Slow-acting – adds nutrients and fibre to the soil; more quickly absorbed in warm than cold soil	Dig well into the soil every autumn or winter	5kg/sq m (11lb/sq yd)
Concentrated organic fertilizer (bonemeal, dried blood, fishmeal, poultry manure, wood ash etc.)	Same purpose and speed of absorption as bulky organic matter but is more intensive and contains very little fibre	As a base dressing, dig into soil before planting in winter or spring, or apply as a top-dressing around plants at any time	50-200g/sq m (2-8oz/sq yd)
Inorganic fertilizer	Mainly quick-acting; highly concentrated source of nutrients	**Granular and powdered forms:** as a base dressing dig into soil at planting time; as a topdressing apply once a year (generally in spring but check instructions) **Liquid forms:** as a foliar feed apply regularly in growing season	15-30g/sq m ($\frac{1}{2}$-1oz/sq yd)
Hydrated or garden lime	Slow-acting; improves texture of heavy soil; corrects soil acidity	As a topdressing apply after digging, in autumn	450g/sq m (1lb/sq yd)

Watering

Water is essential for all plant growth, although some plants have adapted to drought conditions – cacti and succulents, for example, survive for many months on little water. If you live in a climate with low rainfall it is important to choose plants that will tolerate dry conditions, unless you are able to spend time and thought on watering systems. Roof gardens and other sites exposed to drying winds increase the watering needs of your plants.

A variety of watering systems and devices are available to help you, notably drip-watering systems and water-retaining granules. It is best to water at dawn or dusk when the sun's rays are less powerful and the evaporation rate is much reduced. To encourage deep roots to develop, water thoroughly and regularly rather than little and more often, especially when watering lawns.

Watering plants grown in a raised bed
Plants grown in raised beds or containers need more watering. Choose drought-tolerant plants that grow best in free-draining soils.

Easy-watering systems

In any garden, easy access to water is imperative. An outdoor garden tap is vital, unless the kitchen tap is easily accessible. Also essential is a hosepipe long enough to reach the furthest corners of the garden.

In times of drought, however, water may be rationed and you may well have to recycle washing water from the house. Installing a water butt to collect run-off rainwater is a sensible precaution. Large areas of grass are particularly vulnerable to drought, and although sprinkler systems can be installed to aid watering, you may well find that at the very time your lawn needs water most, you are banned from using watering equipment!

There are some simple systems available which deliver water to the garden, as needed, at the flick of a switch. If you have a small garden in a warm climate, or if you garden on an exposed

A seephose laid under a shrub
The diagram above shows the benefits of a seephose. You can see how the water is concentrated directly in the root area, with no wastage.

site, such as a roof terrace, consider planning a seephose or drip-feed system, which can be laid permanently in the planting areas.

Drip-feed systems
This consists of a series of fine bore pipes, with drip heads at intervals, that you

can position exactly where water is required – at the foot of plants needing frequent watering, for example. A soil-moisture detector can be fitted to the system, ensuring that the automatic system is overridden if the ground is sufficiently damp. Drip-feed systems tend to get blocked

with debris, so it is important to clean the system regularly.

Seephose system
This is useful for watering large areas, such as lawns, or for rows of vegetables. It is an efficient way of using water because it is directed straight at the roots. The hose is punctured with a series of fine holes so that a regular, even supply of water is delivered over the length of the hose. A similar system uses a porous hosepipe. The system can be buried beneath the soil to make it both permanent and unobtrusive.

Water take-up
A regular supply of water must reach a plant's roots. Here a drip feed delivers a steady flow.

How to water containers

Plants in containers lose water very rapidly through evaporation. Terracotta pots especially are notoriously poor at retaining moisture. Hanging baskets, with their small amount of soil and large area exposed to the elements, are very greedy for water and may well need watering once a day in hot weather.

Group containers together to preserve moisture, and have them in shade in hot weather.

Watering the root base
To make sure water penetrates the compost, make a few holes around the edge of the pot with a cane before watering.

Reviving a wilting plant
If a plant is wilting from lack of water, plunge it into a bowl of water so that the pot is covered. Leave it until air bubbles subside.

Watering hanging baskets
To make watering high-level hanging baskets easier, attach a cane to the end of a hose to create a rigid, elongated spout.

Retaining moisture

A major difficulty with growing plants in containers is keeping the plants supplied with water, especially when using loamless composts as these are very difficult to re-wet after drying out. To overcome this, add granules of polymer to the compost. When wetted, these granules swell to form a moisture-retaining gel which can hold vast amounts of water. The water is gradually released into the compost.

1 *When planting, add polymer granules to the compost to help hold in water.*

2 *Water so that granules swell, then add remaining compost before planting up as usual.*

Making the most of water

There are various ways to reduce the need for watering. First and foremost, you need to increase the moisture-retaining properties of the soil, if it is sandy, by adding plenty of organic matter. Secondly, you need to reduce the amount of water lost through evaporation, by screening your plants from the effects of drying winds.

Grouping plants together helps to reduce evaporation, as does using pebbles or stones over the soil surface. Containers, in particular, benefit from having the surface covered with pebbles. and from standing close together on a pebble surface. To keep plants moist, stand the container on a bed of pebbles in a tray of water.

Gravel base
To reduce moisture loss, stand the plants on moist pebbles.

Drought-resistant plants

If you live in a very dry climate with free-draining soil, you need to make sure your plants are as drought-resistant as possible, to give the plants the best chance of success and to save you from spending a great deal of time watering. Generally speaking, apart from those succulent plants which store water in their tissue (either in their leaves or stem), plants that are tolerant of drought can be recognized by their foliage. It is usually silvery-grey, finely divided and sometimes covered in fine hairs or felt, all of which reduce evaporation. The following plants are all happy in dry conditions.

Agapanthus spp.
Agave spp.
Aloe spp.
Artemisia spp.
Buddleja davidii
Buxus sempervirens
Campsis radicans
Clivia miniata
Convolvulus cneorum
Crassula spp.
Cynara cardunculus
Eryngium giganteum

Hedera spp.
Lavandula angustifolia
L. spica
Pelargonium species and cultivars
Phormium tenax
Sedum spp.
Sempervivum spp.
Brachyglottis greyi (*Senecio greyi*)
Stachys lanata
Verbascum bonariensis

Agave utahensis

Digging

When you dig, you are creating better growing conditions for your plants. Digging opens up the soil and lets in air, which allows organic matter to break down more easily and release nutrients. It also improves drainage and encourages plants to form deeper root systems. As you dig, you have the opportunity to add manure or compost to the soil and to remove perennial weeds, or to bury annual weeds and other plant debris. All will add nutrients to the soil.

As a general rule, autumn is the best time to dig, especially if you are working on a heavy, clay soil. At this time of year the soil should be perfect for cultivation,

neither too wet nor too hard. Leave the soil roughly dug over the winter months, so that the frost and rain can break down the larger clods of earth and improve the soil texture. Never dig the ground when it is frozen or waterlogged, as this severely damages the soil structure.

There are three different digging techniques. In **simple digging** a spadeful of soil is lifted and inverted as it is dropped back into its original position. In **single digging** the soil is cultivated to the depth of one spade, using a trench system, and in **double digging** the soil is cultivated to the depth of two spades, again working across a plot that has been divided into trenches.

Simple digging

This is the easiest and quickest method, good for clearing shallow-rooted weeds and creating a fine layer of soil on the surface. It is useful when digging in confined spaces and around mature, established plants.

No trench system is involved. Just lift a spadeful of soil and turn it over before dropping it back into its original position. Then break up the soil with the spade, in a brisk, chopping action.

When the ground has been thoroughly dug, leave it for at least three weeks before any planting or seed sowing is carried out. This will allow the soil plenty of time to settle and should be long enough for any buried weeds to be killed. The surface of the soil will start to disintegrate and separate into smaller clods as it is broken down by the various actions of the weather. This will make it much easier to create a fine tilth, with the aid of a fork and a rake.

Using a fork

If the soil is particularly heavy and difficult to penetrate with a spade, it may be easier to use a fork because the soil does not stick to the prongs in the same way that it does to a blade. Fork tines are ideal for breaking down the soil to a finer tilth, and teasing out unwanted plant roots and debris. However, in normal conditions, a spade is better for slicing through the soil and cutting through weeds.

Forking out weeds
A fork is ideal for removing deep-rooted, perennial weeds.

How to dig
Many people dig incorrectly, with the result that the soil is not properly cultivated and they risk back injury.

It is essential to to adopt the correct posture and to use tools that are the right size and comfortable.

In the winter, make sure you are suitably dressed, as cold muscles are prone to injury. Do not dig too hard or too long on the first occasion, and plan the order of work (see opposite).

1 *Insert the spade, vertically, into the soil, with one foot pressing on the blade. Make sure that the handle of the spade is sloping slightly away from you.*

2 *Pull the handle towards you, slide your left hand down the shaft of the spade and bend your knees, slightly, for correct balance, before starting to lever out the soil.*

3 *Lift the soil onto the spade gradually, straightening your legs so that they take the weight and your back is not strained. Work rhythmically and do not lift too much at one time.*

Order of digging

Approach digging work systematically. Mark out the area to be dug with a taut garden line. Move the soil from the first trench to the end of the plot, ready to fill the final trench. Then fill each trench with soil from the next trench to be dug. If the plot seems too big, divide it in half and work each half in turn. This method avoids any unnecessary handling of the soil, which could compact it and possibly damage its structure.

Sequence of work

Work across and then down the plot, as here, so that all of the ground is thoroughly dug.

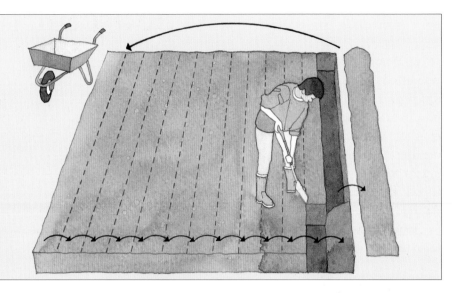

Single digging

This method ensures that an area of ground is thoroughly dug to a consistent depth.

Single digging is usually done with a spade but with heavier soils, a fork can be used. The soil is cultivated to one spade's (or fork's) depth by digging progressive trenches across a plot.

First mark out a trench with a garden line. Dig a trench about 30cm (12in) wide and move the soil from this first trench to the opposite end of the plot. Facing the trench that has

already been dug, dig a second trench and use the soil from this trench to fill in the first trench. Twist the spade or fork a little when putting the soil into the first trench so that the upper layers of the soil, and any weeds, fall to the bottom of the first trench.

Repeat the process down the plot. When the final trench is reached, it is filled with soil from the first trench. You can add manure or compost as you dig. Spread the manure around the trench and then fork it well into the soil.

Digging trenches
Mark out the plot with garden lines. Dig trenches about 30cm (12in) wide and to the depth of the spade or fork.

Filling trenches
Fill in each trench with the soil from the previous trench. For the last trench, use soil removed from the first.

Double digging

This is the deepest method of cultivation, and improves drainage by breaking up any hard pan which has formed in the lower levels of the soil. The trenches are twice as wide as for single digging and a spade and a fork are used.

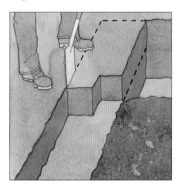

Order of digging

How to double dig

First mark out, with a garden line, the area to be dug, as with single digging.
• Using the spade, dig a trench approximately 60cm (2ft) wide and the depth of the spade. Then remove the soil to the opposite end of the digging area, ready to fill in the final trench.
• Stand in the newly dug trench and break up the bottom soil, using a fork to the depth of its tines (see right). This cultivates the soil to a depth of about 50cm (20in). At this stage, add compost or manure, if required, and fork it into the soil.
• Mark out another trench, parallel to the first one. It is important to get these

measurements accurate and have each trench about the same size. They need to be roughly equal so that the same amount of soil is moved from trench to trench and the ground is kept roughly level. To make this easier, turn, so that you are digging across the trench, and divide it into three sections.
• Dig the second trench, filling the first trench with the soil you have just excavated. Fork the bottom of the trench, as before, and continue to the next trench. Proceed in this way, methodically, across the plot. When you reach the final trench, fill it with the soil dug from the first trench.

Double digging
Stand in each trench that has been dug and, using a fork to the full depth of its tines, break up the lower levels of soil to an overall depth of 50cm (20in). This will improve drainage.

Weed control

A weed is any plant growing in a place where it is not wanted. Many cause problems just because they are so tough and versatile that they can adapt to a wide range of growing conditions. For this reason they must always be dealt with before they get out of control. Weeds compete directly with your garden plants for light, nutrients and water. They can also act as hosts to pests and diseases, which can spread as the season progresses. Groundsel, for instance, often harbours the fungal diseases rust and mildew, and sap-sucking greenfly. Chickweed meanwhile, plays host to red spider mite and whitefly.

Gravel mulch
Covering the soil with a mulch such as gravel will block out light and prevent weed seeds from germinating.

Perennial weeds

Digging up perennial weeds is an effective disposal system, provided that every bit of the root system is removed from the soil. If only a few weeds are present, try digging them out with a knife or trowel, but you must remove the top 5cm (2in) of root close to the surface, to prevent the weed re-growing. This method can be used in the lawn to get rid of individual or small patches of weeds, and is a reliable means of eradicating weeds growing close to garden plants. In this situation, often no other weed control method would be effective without risking damage to plants growing nearby.

Digging up perennials
Some perennial weeds, such as dandelions, have very long and tenacious roots. When digging them out, be sure to remove the whole root, or they will reappear.

Clearing weeds
The simplest way to deal with weeds is to remove them physically, either by pulling or digging them out or, if they are small, hoeing them off at soil level.

The biggest problem with this method of control is that most weed seeds require exposure to light before they will germinate. Often, when weeding disturbs the soil, more air is allowed into the surface layers and an ideal seedbed is created. Although the existing weed seedlings are destroyed, the weed growth cycle starts all over again. This problem is often worse when using rotary cultivators because they leave the surface layers of soil light and fluffy, making a perfect seedbed. Perennial weeds are increased, too, because they are chopped into pieces, each capable of growing.

The most effective way to clear weeds, especially established perennials, is to use a combination of cultural and chemical methods. Spray weeds in full growth with a chemical weedkiller and, as they start to die, bury them when the area is dug over. When the new weed seedlings germinate, spray them with a chemical (see right) while they are most vulnerable.

Annual weeds

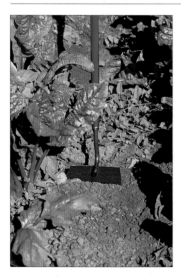

Clearing annual weeds with a hoe is quick and effective, but the timing is important. The hoeing must be done when the weeds are tiny and before they start producing seed.

Hoeing will sever the stems of young weeds from the root system just below

Hoeing annuals
Hoeing on a regular basis, when weeds are still small and have not set seed, is a very quick and efficient method of weed control.

soil level. This both prevents the stem from forming new roots and stops the roots from producing a new stem. When hoeing, make sure you always walk backwards to avoid treading weeds back into the soil.

There is an old saying, 'One year's seeds make seven years' weeds', which has now been endorsed by scientific research and proved to be remarkably accurate, unfortunately for gardeners.

Annual weeds are capable of producing a staggering total of 60,000 viable seeds per square metre, per year. The vast majority of these seeds are found in the uppermost 5cm (2in) of soil, but they will usually germinate only when exposed to sufficient light levels. This is why mulching, which covers the soil and blocks out light, has become such a widely popular method of weed control. The added benefit of mulching is that there is little chance of contaminating the soil with chemical residue.

Mulching for weed control

Mulching is the practice of covering the soil around plants with a layer of material to block out the light and help trap moisture. In today's gardens, where plastics are commonplace, inorganic black plastic sheeting is often chosen. Though not inviting to look at, it can be hidden beneath a thin layer of more attractive organic mulch.

As a general rule, organic mulches provide the bonus of improving the fertility of the soil, but inorganic mulches are more effective because they form a better weed barrier. To be fully effective as a barrier, organic mulches must be applied as a layer at least 10cm (4in) thick. Both organic and inorganic mulches tend to be less effective against established perennial weeds, unless an entire area can be sealed until the weeds have died out and planting is carried out through the mulch while it is in place. One way of clearing weedy ground in summer is to cover the soil with a mulch of clear or white plastic, sealed around the edges. Weeds are gradually killed by a combination of high temperatures and lack of carbon dioxide.

The plastic can be removed and used elsewhere and the treated area is weed-free, ready to plant and cover with an organic mulch, such as shredded bark or gravel.

Black plastic mulch
Onions are planted through a black plastic mulch. This is a very useful and labour-saving method of suppressing weed growth.

Chemical weed control

Any chemical which is used to kill weeds is a herbicide. Herbicides are preferred by some gardeners as a labour-saving alternative to cultural weed control. They are certainly the most effective method of controlling persistent, perennial weeds, once they have become established. When using any type of chemical weedkiller, do not, ever, exceed the recommended dosage and always handle with care. The weedkillers are grouped into three categories according to the way they work.
Contact These are chemicals which are applied to the leaves and stems of weeds, and they will only injure and kill those specific parts. This type of weedkiller is most effective when it is used to control annual weeds, and especially seedlings.
Residual These are 'soil acting' chemicals which are applied to the soil. They may persist in the soil for some months before they are taken up by the roots of the weeds, and the whole weed will slowly die.
Systemic These chemicals are applied to the leaves and stems of the weeds and are absorbed into the weed by being transported through sap. In time, they injure and kill the whole weed. This type of weedkiller is the most effective one for controlling perennial weeds, especially if the weeds are established.

Applying systemic weed killer
Any chemical sprays should be applied in cool, windless weather, when the leaves are dry. Follow instructions on chemical container carefully and always wear recommended protective clothing.

Plant controls

Certain plants may be able to combat weeds by competing with them. They need the following characteristics:
• A low, spreading habit, so that the soil surface is shaded.
• Evergreen or coniferous foliage to keep the soil covered in the spring, when most weed seeds germinate.
• A fast growth rate to cover an area as quickly as possible, and outgrow the weeds.
• The adaptability to cope with a range of growing conditions, with very little care and maintenance.

The soil must be weed-free before planting begins.

Ground cover planting
Periwinkle (Vinca) is an ideal ground-cover plant, as it is evergreen, low-growing and does well in shady parts of the garden.

Reclaiming a neglected garden

The treatment used for reclaiming a garden will depend on a number of factors, such as how long the garden has been left uncultivated, how overgrown the area is and whether there are any existing plants that are worth saving.

Where woody perennials such as brambles are the main problem, the best approach is to cut down all the weed vegetation to ground level, in late winter or early spring, in order to stimulate the development of new growth.

When the new growth is about 45cm (18in) high, spray the weeds with a systemic weedkiller, which will quickly be absorbed, through the soft, new leaves and stems, down into the root system. Within six weeks, even the most tenacious of woody, perennial weeds should be dead or severely damaged.

The soil can now be cultivated to remove the dead and dying weeds and to bring the soil back into good condition. For non-woody perennials the treatment is the same, but the weeds can be buried within two weeks of spraying and they will die in the soil.

Use a follow-up spray to kill germinated seedlings.

Supporting plants

Many plants will need help from you, the gardener, to be seen at their best, and in some instances, to prevent them being damaged by strong winds and heavy rainstorms. Support young trees with slender stems for the first couple of years, until they are strong and well established. Usually a stout, wooden support (see opposite) inserted at planting will do the job. Climbers and wall shrubs, depending on their type and their natural clinging abilities, also need some form of tying in, or supporting, with a wooden trellis or a system of wires nailed to the supporting wall. Tall perennials with thin or lax stems, such as delphiniums, or heavy heads of flowers, such as peonies, require some assistance, too. The best way to deal with them is with a wire or brushwood cage, or a surrounding framework of peasticks.

High summer border
A traditional herbaceous border, designed with taller flowers at the back. Many taller plants need support, so stake them while they are still small and accessible. New growth soon obscures the supports.

Types of support

The equipment available for staking is shown below. What you need will depend on the dimensions of the plant you have chosen to grow but, in principle, make sure that the stake is strong enough for its purpose and that the tie allows room for the plant to grow without cutting into the main stem and damaging it. For perennials, ensure that any support is as unobtrusive as possible, so as not to detract from the flowers. Natural wood and green-coloured stakes blend better into planting than brightly coloured plastic ones. To avoid injury, always make sure you cover the ends of bare canes with plastic tops.

Container plants
Container plants need supports that complement them. Bulbs that tend to flop, like daffodils or hyacinths, can be given cages made of natural materials – canes, brushwood or willow stems. Container-grown climbers can twine over small trellis fans, and ivies can be trained on metal hoops to create a form of instant topiary. Wigwams of canes, tied at the top, are ideal for climbing annuals.

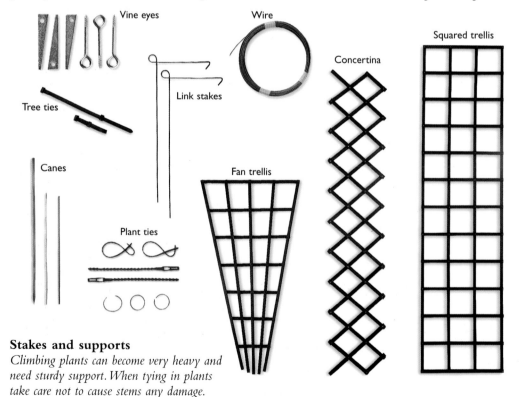

Stakes and supports
Climbing plants can become very heavy and need sturdy support. When tying in plants take care not to cause stems any damage.

Fan trellis

Tree supports

Trees with weak or developing stems may need support until they are well established. A stake, long enough to reach just below the crown, will protect the roots from strong winds. Stake container-grown or rootballed trees at a 45° angle, which clears the rootball, causing no damage. Hammer stakes down so that they penetrate by a third of their overall height.

Young trees
A short stake holds the stem of the tree firmly in the first year.

Older trees
Use a taller stake (to just below the crown) and two ties.

Container-grown trees
Use an angled stake to avoid damaging the rootball.

Supports for climbers

Form dictates the kind of support that will best suit your climbing plants. Those that climb with aerial roots need no help from you, the gardener, as they are self-attaching. Those with twining stems, such as honeysuckle, will need trellis or wires around which their leading shoots can twist, while those that merely scramble will need to be actively tied into an appropriate support.

The support can be unobtrusive or decorative. A wigwam of canes or poles for climbing, flowering annuals like sweet peas, or vegetables like runner beans, can be very eye-catching.

Make sure there is a gap between any wooden support and the surface to which it is attached, to enable air to circulate freely behind the plant, which will help to prevent diseases. Trellis attached to surfaces in need of annual coats of preservative or paint should be hinged at the base. The entire trellis can then be dismounted from the wall once a year, with the plant still *in situ*, and lowered to the ground while the essential maintenance work takes place.

Wires can be strung along, using vine eyes at intervals, leaving a gap of about 5cm (2in) between the wires and the wall. The wire-supporting structure will vary according to the habit of the plant. For fruiting plants that are trained in a fan you will need to have a horizontal wire system to which the branches can be tied at 45cm (18in) intervals.

Tree ties
The best ties are made of thick material that does not cut into the plant's stem, with notches so that it can be let out as the plant's girth increases. A spacer also helps to prevent the tie chafing on the bark. Make sure the tie is secured loosely enough to allow room for growth, and check it every six months to see if it needs releasing.

The tie should be fixed near the top of the stake, ensuring that there is adequate room to prevent chafing.

Supports for perennials and shrubs

Perennial plants vary in how much propping up they need. Tall perennials or shrubs with weak stems will not stay upright without support, and the best systems to use are those that are unobtrusive and loosely support the plant without restricting its growth. To avoid the expense of buying stakes, surround the plant with a low 'fence' of well-branched twigs.

Purpose-made ring stakes are available in various forms. Those that consist of a rigid structure, rather than a clipped one, should be placed in position before the plant is too well-grown, otherwise you risk snapping off any delicate stems.

Trellis support
A natural wood trellis provides support for a Virginia creeper.

Wire support
Horizontal wires attached to a wall support this wisteria.

Link stakes
Metal link stakes can improve the shape of soft-stemmed plants, like this pelargonium.

Twig stakes
Canes and string can be used to train flopping plants with woody stems, like this fuchsia.

Lawns

The lawn is frequently dismissed as merely, a flat, green expanse requiring a great deal of work for little reward. However, often the largest single area in the garden, it has an important contribution to make. A healthy, well-maintained lawn makes an attractive area to play or relax in, as well as setting off beds and borders. The most important aspect of lawn care is to grow the appropriate grass for your soil. No amount of care can make a suitable lawn in the wrong situation. When selecting seed, bear in mind the purpose your lawn will serve. An ornamental lawn has fine grass, a child's play area, tougher, hardwearing grasses, and where trees are a focal point in the lawn, the grass needs to be shade-tolerant.

Informal lawn
In large gardens, particularly in orchards, the grass can be much less carefully tended. Tougher meadow grasses are ideal.

Mowing

If you wish to maintain a neat, healthy lawn, regular mowing is very important as it helps the grass to divide and so thicken. Cut little and often, and do not cut more than one-third of a blade in length at any one time. Infrequent mowing allows coarser grass to predominate. Mow most frequently in warm, moist conditions, but keep mowing to a minimum in hot, dry weather. Never allow the grass to grow more than about 4cm (1$\frac{1}{2}$in) long. Cutting too close weakens the grass and produces bare patches, which encourages moss and weeds.

As a rough guide, ornamental lawns should be mown to between 1.5-2cm ($\frac{1}{2}$–$\frac{3}{4}$in) to keep the grass growing well. Allow lawns intended for more wear and tear to grow slightly longer, normally to about 2–2.5cm ($\frac{3}{4}$–1in) long to enable it to withstand heavy foot traffic.

The choice of mower is largely a matter of personal preference. It does not matter which type of mower you have, provided that the blades are sharp and adjusted to obtain the best cutting action. The striped lawn effect some gardeners prefer is made by the roller on a lawn mower and not by the blades.

In hot, dry weather, raise the height of the cut by about 1.5cm ($\frac{1}{2}$in). This is done to shade the roots and to reduce water evaporation. Remove all grass cuttings, to control pests and disease and discourage worms.

An ornamental lawn
A mown and rollered lawn with fine-leaved grasses does not stand hard wear but looks marvellous.

Mowing over stones
Stones set in a lawn to form a path should be placed below the level of the turf for easy mowing.

Mowing actions
Rotary and hover mowers cut with a scything action, whereas cylinders cut like scissors. The former is useful for informal lawns, the latter for formal, close-cut lawns.

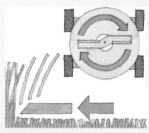

Rotary mower action

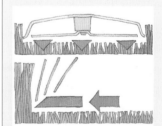

Hover mower action

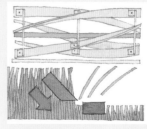

Cylinder mower action

Routine lawn care

If the lawn feels soft and spongy it is probably due to a layer of dead grass clippings – 'thatch' – which has formed on the soil surface. If left, this layer may harbour pests and diseases, as well as weed seeds.

For light layers of thatch, a spring-tine rake is ideal for dragging out the dead material from the soil surface. Remove this waste from the lawn for the raking to be really beneficial. Where thatch has built up to form a thick layer, it is best to scarify the lawn using a spring-tined machine to rip out the dead grass. Set the scarifier up so that the tines penetrate the soil surface and prune the grass roots.

Troublesome lawn weeds are likely to be those with a rosette or spreading habit. Remove them with a sharp knife, or control them with a hormone-type weedkiller applied in spring or autumn.

Moss is encouraged when the grass is growing slowly, usually because of poor drainage and shade. Shading is often caused by leaves lying over the surface in the autumn. This problem is best controlled by raking the lawn vigorously to a depth of 1.5cm (½in) with a fan rake. Always rake from the edges to the centre of the mossy area to help reduce the risk of moss spreading into parts of the lawn which are not affected. Never compost moss, as some may survive and spread again.

Raking up moss
A fan rake is an ideal tool for raking up dead moss and compacted, dead, grass clippings. Rake from the edges to the centre to avoid spreading the moss.

Watering

In an average year, most well-kept lawns only need watering for about two to three months, but occasionally there are dry periods when the soil water reserves are not sufficient. A lawn only needs watering when signs of water stress become visible. The usual signs are grass blades taking on a dull sheen, often with a bluish tint, and footprints that are easy to see as the grass is limp and does not spring back into position. The way in which water is applied is more important than the quantity of water: always ensure the lawn is given a good soaking. Frequent, light applications in dry weather encourages shallow rooting and makes the grass more vulnerable if watering is discontinued. In very dry conditions, it is better to use a slow-running hose to soak the lawn rather than a sprinkler which is not as effective.

Lawn sprinkler
Regular lawn watering is easier with a sprinkler, which needs to be moved to cover larger areas.

Problem solving

Fungal diseases of grasses can cause severe lawn damage. These are worst in autumn when damp conditions tend to favour their development.

A well-maintained lawn can usually withstand most pests and diseases. Surface signs of lawn problems are generally symptoms of grass root problems.

The most common cause of poor growth or disease is grass roots being deprived of oxygen because the soil is compacted and the air pressed out of it. This causes a slow-down in root activity which means the top growth of the lawn becomes weak and unhealthy. Overcome this by aerating the lawn.

Naturalizing a lawn

You may like to try and encourage wild flowers to establish themselves and grow in longer grass, creating more of a meadow than a lawn. Even if you do so, the grass will still need some cutting, roughly speaking about twice each year. A sickle copes better than a mower with longer, woody grass of this sort, and is ideal for cutting grass to 15cm (6in) in autumn.

Using a sickle
Longer grass becomes woody in a naturalized lawn and the easiest way to cut it is to use a sickle.

Lawn repair

Due to the mass of roots beneath grass, it is possible to cut and lift sections of turf and treat them like sections of living carpet. Light damage, such as broken edges to the lawn, can be repaired, quite easily, by cutting out a section of turf that includes the damaged edge and turning it so that the damaged section lies within the lawn. Sow grass seed in the damaged part.

1 *To repair a broken edge cut out a section of turf including the damaged edge. Slice through the root system of the turf.*

2 *Lift the turf free of the soil. Turn it round and re-lay it so that the damaged edge is in the lawn. Firm the turf into position.*

3 *Fill the hole created by the broken edge with fine soil and sow grass seed. Germination should take 10-14 days.*

Increasing plants

It is both satisfying and economical to create beautiful displays in the garden by growing new plants from seeds and cuttings, or by dividing old, established clumps to form young, healthy plants. Many methods of propagation are very simple, once certain principles are grasped, and they require little equipment. Once you have gained some experience, a simple propagator and a cold frame will allow you to grow wonderful summer bedding displays and a much wider range of plants than is available in the garden centre. An added bonus is that you can easily swap plants with friends and neighbours.

Young chamomile plants
Growing new plants from seed is an easy, and inexpensive, way to increase plant stocks.

What is propagation?

Propagation is the use of seeds or other parts of living plants to produce more plants. This process can be carried out in two ways – either by seed or vegetatively.

Seed is a sexual method of reproduction where the seed develops following the fertilization of the female part of the plant by male pollen. Vegetative propagation is an asexual method and includes taking cuttings of stem or leaf, dividing rootstock, layering or grafting in order to produce more plants.

Sowing seed is the easiest and most reliable method of producing large numbers of plants quickly. Plants grown from seed are also, generally speaking, healthier and more disease-resistant.

Some plants, however, do not produce viable seed. The seeds may take a long time to reach flowering age, or do not breed true, which means that the seedlings can differ greatly from the parent plant in form, habit and flower colour. This variation allows many new and improved plants to be produced. However, in cases where an exact replica of the parent plant is desired, for instance, in the propagation of especially fine forms of plants or of variegated plants, a vegetative method of propagation is used. This is the only way to be sure that any plant produced is identical in all its features to the parent plant.

Choosing suitable plant material

Always choose cuttings or collect seed from the strongest and heathiest plants available to give the best possible chance of successful propagation. Poor plants provide inferior material, and are rarely transformed into sturdy, new plants.

Seed
Choose the best-formed fruits or seedheads and be aware that timing is critical when collecting seed. If you leave it too late, the seed will already have been dispersed, and if you gather seeds too early, they will not germinate. Gather seed on a dry day and if there is any dampness put them in the sun to dry thoroughly. If you are not sowing them immediately, store them in a cool, dry place out of direct sunlight. If you are buying in seed, select packets which are undamaged and which have the most recent datestamp, as old seed does not germinate so well.

Cuttings
Take cuttings from thriving plants and discard any thin, weak shoots. It is best to choose non-flowering shoots, as these regenerate more readily than older or flowering shoots. If you have to take cuttings of flowering stems, remove any flowers so that all the energy goes into producing roots. Choose shoots from the current year's growth, as this is the most vigorous plant material.

Collecting seeds
Hang thoroughly dry seedheads in a plastic bag to collect seeds.

Taking cuttings
Choose only strong, healthy shoots for making cuttings.

Encouraging root formation
Hormone rooting powder can be used on the cut surface of a cutting to promote root development. There are varying strengths to suit different types of cutting. Follow the manufacturer's instructions.

Rooting powder
Dip only the cut ends of the cuttings in hormone powder before planting.

The propagation environment

Creating the right environment is the key to producing new plants. During propagation, plants are extremely vulnerable. It is therefore essential to provide a protected environment which reduces stress for the young plants and increases their chance of survival. Keeping seeds and seedlings in warm, humid conditions encourages rapid germination as well as healthy growth.

Leafy cuttings, when first taken, have no roots. To prevent them from wilting and encourage the speedy formation of new roots, they need to be in an environment with high humidity. This can be created very simply and cheaply by growing seeds on a warm windowsill, or by raising cuttings in a pot enclosed within a plastic bag. Hold the bag clear of the cuttings with sticks – the leaves will rot if they come into contact with the moisture that collects on the plastic. The addition of bottom heat is necessary for the germination of certain seeds, such as half-hardy annuals, and for the successful rooting of some cuttings. There are various heated units available (see below).

When cuttings and seedlings are ready to leave the protected environment of a propagating unit, they must be very gradually accustomed to the changes in humidity and air temperature – a process that is known as hardening off (see p. 96).

Propagating equipment

There is a range of propagating equipment available to suit any gardener's needs, from basic seed trays to thermostatically controlled mist-propagation units.

A plastic propagator is useful for propagating seeds and cuttings in summer and there are units small enough to fit on a windowsill. Propagating units with their own heat supply speed up rooting and germinating and are necessary for some seeds and cuttings. There are also heating bases that can be bought separately, for placing underneath your seed trays.

If you plan to propagate many plants, it is worth your while investing in a cold frame. The advantages of a frame are that the soil and air temperatures are warmer than open ground and the humidity is higher. Frames are particularly useful as an intermediate stage for 'hardening' plants, so they can be moved gradually from a warm, protected environment to an outdoor site without suffering.

Heated electric propagator
This propagating unit with room for three seed trays has an electric base with an adjustable thermostatic control for flexible temperatures. The rigid lid retains heat.

Degradable containers
You can replant seedlings grown in these containers directly into soil without disturbing the roots.

Plant hygiene
The warm, damp, enclosed space of a propagation environment is an ideal breeding ground for air- and water-borne spores of fungi and bacteria which attack and often kill plants. Always use new or well-scrubbed pots and seed trays. Clean tools regularly and dip them in a solution of methylated spirit between cuttings. Water the propagator with a fungicidal solution once it is planted up.

Bad practice
An encrusted and unwashed pots is a breeding ground for bacteria and fungi.

Cold frame
A cold frame is a great boon in propagation. This model has a sliding glass lid to adjust ventilation when acclimatizing plants, or airing new plants on warm days. Frames are useful for propagating and hardening off plants and for over-wintering alpines that suffer from winter wet.

Seed tray fitted with hoops
Make a simple and inexpensive portable propagating unit by forming wire into hoops over a seed tray. Insert the tray into a clear polythene bag to create a humid atmosphere. The hoops ensure that the leaves do not touch the polythene.

Growing from seed

Growing new plants from seed is the most common, and possibly the easiest, method of propagating a large number of plants quickly. It is ideal for growing plants for bedding displays and containers, and for filling gaps in summer borders. There is great variation between seeds, not only in terms of size and outer covering, but also in the time it takes for them to germinate, and their success rate. The growth rate of seedlings also varies. Plants need specific conditions for their seeds to achieve successful germination. Some of them prefer cool, light conditions, while others need warmth and darkness to trigger growth. Always store seed in a cool, airy place and make sure that you know the individual requirements of a particular seed before you sow it.

Preparing seed

A seed is a complete plant in embryo, but it is in a resting phase. Certain seeds need preliminary treatment to speed up germination.

Soaking seeds
To aid germination soak hard seeds in water to soften the seed coat.

Scraping seeds
Put small, hard seeds in a jar lined with sandpaper and shake the jar.

Chipping seeds
Nick the outer coat of large hard-coated seed with a sharp knife.

Scarification

Seeds with very hard coats take a long time to germinate unless you break down the seed coat so the seed can absorb moisture. This treatment is called scarification. The easiest method is to soak the seeds in warm water for 24 hours. Where the seed coat is very hard, you may have to wear it down in one of two ways:
Scraping Place small seeds in a jar lined with sandpaper and shake the jar.
Chipping Using a sharp knife, make a nick in the outer coat of large seeds.

Do not damage the inner, soft material, the part of the seed that will germinate, or the seed may rot.

Stratification

Use stratification for seeds encased in fleshy fruits, such as hips and berries. It allows the fruit to rot away without the seeds drying out.

Place some broken pieces of flowerpot in a large pot, add 50cm (20in) of sand or seed compost, then a layer of seeds, then another 50cm (20in) of sand or compost. Repeat until the pot is almost full, and finish with a layer of sand. Store in a cool, moist spot outside, and turn the mixture from time to time.

Low temperatures

Some seeds only germinate after exposure to low temperatures of 5° C (41° F) or less, in winter. In the spring, the seeds can be sown in the normal way.

Sowing outdoors

The seeds of hardy perennials and hardy annuals are normally sown out of doors. These seeds can be sown in their final flowering position to avoid transplanting. The best time to sow them is four weeks after the last severe frost in mainland Europe and the USA, or mid-spring in the UK. Check the instructions on the seed packet. Make sure that the soil has warmed up; if it is cold, many seeds will rot.

Prepare the seedbed by digging well in autumn and adding peat or other organic matter at the rate of one cubic metre to every four square metres of soil. On heavy soils, incorporate grit or sand to open it up and improve drainage. A raised bed helps drainage, allowing the soil to warm up more quickly. Now sow the seeds as described in the steps below.

1 *Tread the soil to form a firm surface. Use a rake to remove stones and make a level surface with a fine, crumbly texture.*

2 *Use a taut garden line for guidance on where to sow. Draw the corner of a rake or hoe along the ground to make a drill.*

3 *Sow seeds thinly in the drill, either singly or in groups of two or three. Cover the seeds with a fine layer of soil using the rake.*

4 *Seeds can be watered in after sowing if a very fine spray is used. Alternatively, water the bed the day before you plan to start.*

Sowing under protection

The seeds of more tender plants, such as half-hardy annuals and biennials, need artificial warmth because they will not survive outside in areas where late spring frosts occur. Most of these seeds need temperatures between about 10–21°C (50–70°F) to germinate, but some need high temperatures. To raise the temperature and retain moisture, cover the newly sown seeds with a sheet of glass or with a plastic bag. Your seed packet will give exact instructions as to temperatures required.

Sow seeds in either pots or trays. Plastic containers are the best, being easy to clean and sterilize. Degradable containers are good for large seeds. The seeds are sown directly into a small pot or similar container where they germinate and grow until temperatures are right for planting out. The containers should be planted directly into the soil.

Follow instructions for the depth at which to sow seed. In general, if the seed needs dark to germinate (and not all seeds do) it should only be covered with its own depth of compost. Sow fine and medium-sized seeds evenly in a broadcast fashion over the compost. Space larger seeds at regular intervals. Always label your seeds after sowing.

Germinating seeds
Place seeds in good light in warmth. Cress seedlings germinate very quickly in these conditions.

Sowing fine seeds

1 *Fill the tray with a good seed compost. Firm the soil to within 1.5cm (¹/₂in) of the top. Scatter fine and medium-sized seeds evenly on the surface.*

2 *If the seed needs dark conditions to germinate, use a fine sieve to cover the seed with the required amount of compost. Do not cover the seed too deeply.*

3 *Stand the tray in a shallow bowl of water until the compost surface moistens. Leave to drain. Cover the tray with a glass sheet and place it somewhere warm.*

Seed viability
The length of time that seeds are viable – or capable of germination – varies. Some are viable for one season only. Most last for a year after harvesting, and many are viable for several years. Some (eg *Paeonia*) can take three years to germinate. If in doubt, check before proceeding further.

Sowing large seeds

1 *For easier handling, sow large seeds in a container. Fill the pot with seed compost and level off the top, removing any surplus.*

2 *To ensure that there are no air pockets in the soil, gently firm and level the compost with a flat-bottomed utensil, like a glass.*

3 *Make sure there is a space between the top of the compost and the pot rim, and then sow the seeds evenly on the surface.*

4 *Cover the seed with a layer of compost if it needs darkness to germinate. Water the pot from below and cover it with glass.*

Care of seedlings

Seedlings must be carefully tended as they are still at a vulnerable stage. Remove glass covers as soon as any shoots are visible and make sure the seedlings are not exposed to any drastic changes in their growing conditions. Protect them from draughts and from very bright sunlight. Make sure that roots never dry out. It is usual practice to sow more seeds than you need so that you can select the healthiest seedlings. To prevent overcrowding, thin out the seedlings. You should remove the weakest surplus plants, which compete for light and nutrients, as soon as they are large enough to handle comfortably, leaving the others to grow on.

Pricking out

Prick out a seedling when it develops its first pair of 'true' leaves (see right) and can be handled with ease. Transfer the seedling to an individual pot, or put three seedlings in a larger pot, so that they have the space and depth of soil to grow into a plant. This must be done very carefully to avoid damaging the seedling, which should never be held by its stem.

1 *Using a plant label, lift each seedling carefully with roots intact, holding the seedling by the leaf and never by the stem.*

2 *Make a hole in moistened soil with a dibber and insert the seedling to the same depth as before. Gently firm in the soil.*

Outdoor thinning
Thin outdoor seedlings when the soil is nice and moist to reduce the amount of root disturbance.

'True' leaves
Recognizing the 'true' leaves on a seedling means that you can tell when to move it. The first leaves to appear are the seed leaves (cotyledons), which swell on germination and force the seedcoat open. These leaves should not be handled. Wait to thin out or repot seedlings until the second pair of leaves emerge and are large enough to hold easily. These 'true' leaves are more complex in shape and look more like the leaves of the adult plant.

The seed leaves will appear first, but wait until the 'true' leaves develop before pricking out seedlings.

Hardening off

Any seedlings that have been grown in a warm, protected environment must grow accustomed to harsher outdoor conditions for a period of about two weeks before it is safe to transplant them outside. The usual method is to move the plants outside when they are well established and place them in an unheated cold frame so that they are still protected by glass or polythene. Gradually increase the amount of ventilation by opening or removing the cover, slightly at first, and then for increasingly long periods, until the plants are acclimatized. Close the frame if there is any threat of a frost at night.

Hardening off
Gradually increase the amount of ventilation in a cold frame in order to acclimatize seedlings.

Potting up

As young plants start to grow and need more space, they should be transferred from a smaller pot to a larger one, to avoid the roots becoming cramped and to provide more nutrients in the new soil.

There is no hard and fast rule about the size of the new pot, but it should be big enough to allow a layer of new compost to be placed around the existing rootball. Do not choose a pot that is a great deal bigger than the original one, as this may cause root problems.

Before transplanting, let the plant become slightly dry so that the rootball slides out of the old pot easily, with minimal root disturbance. Hold the plant by the stem and turn the pot upside down to extract the plant. Fill the new pot with a drainage layer and fresh compost. Tap it on a hard surface to make sure that there are no air pockets and then insert the plant to the same depth as before. Finally, firm it well in.

1 *With the stem of the plant securely between your fingers, and your hand over the soil, ease the plant from its old pot.*

2 *Insert the plant in the new pot, filling spaces with new compost and firming it in gently. Water, and leave it to drain.*

Increasing bulbs

Bulbs can be grown from seed, but it may take as many as six or seven years before the seedlings will flower. For this reason, it is often preferable to use the propagating methods of scaling and scoring. These methods also ensure that the new plants are identical to the parent plant, in contrast to seed-raised plants which are variable in character. One of the major attractions of propagating plants, such as lilies, by scaling is that you can remove up to 80 per cent of a mature bulb's scales for propagation. When planted, the parent bulb, itself, will still produce flowers in the following spring.

Naturalized bulbs
When planted in suitable conditions, like these bluebells in woodland, many bulbs will spread and 'naturalize' successfully.

Scaling a bulb

Use this method to propagate scaly bulbs, such as lilies, which have relatively small, narrow scales that can readily be broken away from the base of the bulb. In the autumn, pull the scales away from the base of a bulb. Place the scales in a polythene bag and add an equal amount of moist peat or sand, and a small amount of fungicidal powder to prevent the scales from rotting. Mix the contents together and expel the air by gently squeezing the bag. Then tie the top, loosely, and label it with the plant name and date. Place the bag in a warm dark room for 12-14 weeks. By the end of this time each scale should have formed at least one embryo bulb, complete with small roots. Plant up each new bulb into a small pot.

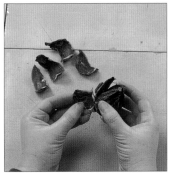

1 *In autumn, break off the outer scales from the base of a bulb, discarding any that are damaged. Mix them with peat and fungicide in a polythene bag.*

2 *Leave the sealed bag in a dark room for 12–14 weeks. After this time, the scales will have developed at least one embryo bulb, complete with small roots.*

3 *Check each scale and bulblet in the bag and if two or more bulblets have developed from the same scale leaf split them apart with a sharp knife.*

4 *Fill small pots with a suitable potting compost. Plant the embryo bulbs singly, or in groups.so that they are just below the compost level.*

Scoring a bulb

This is the most common method of propagation for bulbs, such as hyacinths, whose scale leaves do not readily break away, and which are slow to propagate. In autumn, after the bulbs have been lifted and cleaned, score the base of a bulb to make a series of grooves up to one-third the depth of the bulb. Half fill a pot with loose sand or compost and press the base of the bulb into it. Add more compost until only about the top quarter of the bulb is visible. By the following autumn, young bulblets should have formed. Transplant the bulblets into small pots, or directly into the ground if you prefer.

Scoring a bulb
Using a sharp knife, score the base of a hyacinth bulb by making a series of V-shaped grooves up to one-third the depth of the bulb. Then plant the bulb in compost, with the top visible.

Bulbils
Blackish-purple mini-bulbs often form, just above the leaves, on the stem of certain species of lily, including tiger lilies. Harvest the bulbils three weeks after the flowers have finished.

Sow them as you would sow seed, about 1.5cm ($^1/_2$ in) deep, in a tray or pot, and transplant them after a year. After three years they should flower.

Growing from cuttings

Increasing plants by taking cuttings from their stems is a common way to propagate woody plants. Stem cuttings are divided into three main types, according to the maturity of the plant and the time of year that the cuttings are taken.

Softwood cuttings are taken from shoots of the current season's growth as soon as a shoot's base starts to become firm, from late spring until late autumn.

Semi-ripe cuttings are taken from shoots of the current season's growth just as soon as the base of a shoot has turned woody, in late summer and autumn.

Hardwood cuttings are taken from fully mature shoots of the current season's growth of deciduous shrubs, trees and climbers. They are cut from the parent plant immediately after their leaves have fallen, in late autumn and early winter.

Softwood cutting
A cutting of the current season's growth containing mainly soft, immature tissue.

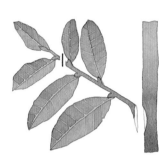

Semi-ripe cutting
A cutting of the current season's growth containing woody tissue at the base.

Hardwood cutting
A cutting of the current season's growth containing woody, fully mature tissue.

Softwood cuttings

There should be minimal delay between removing a softwood cutting from the parent plant and potting it up, because immature stems are very prone to wilting.

Select a vigorous shoot on the parent plant and cut it 7.5–10cm (3–4in) long, with a sharp knife. Protect softwood cuttings, taken outdoors, in a closed plastic bag which should be placed in the shade. Prepare each cutting by trimming the base and stripping away the lower leaves.

Dip just the base in hormone rooting powder and tap the cutting to shake off any excess. Insert at least 5cm (2in) of the stem into a soil-less cuttings compost. Water the pot thoroughly, ideally with sterilized water, preferably containing a fungicide. To prevent wilting, softwood cuttings should be kept in a well-lit, enclosed, damp environment while they initiate roots.

Plants that do not root easily may need bottom heat as well. A heated propagator is best. If you do not have one, simply place a wire hoop or some short canes over the cuttings and cover this with a sealed plastic bag. Every other day, look to see whether the cutting needs water. It should root in 6–8 weeks. Once new growth appears, gradually harden off the cutting.

1 *Cut a strong, young shoot from the parent plant and trim it just below a leaf joint, or node.*

2 *Carefully remove the lower leaves, clearing half the stem for insertion into the compost.*

3 *Fill a small pot with cuttings compost. Dip the cutting in rooting powder, and insert it.*

4 *Water, and cover with a clear plastic bag, forming a mini-greenhouse to retain moisture.*

Semi-ripe cuttings

Semi-ripe cuttings are propagated in a similar way to softwood cuttings, but at a later time of year. The stems of semi-ripe cuttings are therefore harder and more resilient than softwood cuttings. The speed of processing is not quite so critical, because the cuttings will not wilt quite as quickly as softwood cuttings. Semi-ripe cuttings do, however, take longer to initiate roots and therefore various techniques are adopted to improve rooting (see panel, opposite). Unlike softwood cuttings, any soft, sappy growth should be removed from the tip of a semi-ripe cutting before it is inserted into the cuttings compost. Such cuttings should be placed in a propagator or other closed environment while they produce roots. Semi-ripe cuttings, taken in autumn, can be allowed to root slowly over the winter months in a cold frame.

Broadleaved cuttings

A slight variation on the basic method for taking semi-ripe cuttings is used to increase evergreens that have large, broad leaves, often with a thick, leathery texture. Such evergreens can also be propagated over a longer period than semi-ripe cuttings, from mid-autumn to mid-spring. Broadleaved cuttings, 10cm (4in) long, are taken from almost fully mature wood of the current year's growth and are trimmed just below a leaf joint. For flowering plants such as rhododendrons, remove any flower bud in the tip of the cutting. The cutting may, otherwise, develop a flower and not initiate roots. To stimulate a greater number of roots to develop, many broadleaved cuttings benefit from a shallow, angled cut, or wound, made at the base (see panel, right). Because of their leaf size, broadleaved cuttings are often difficult to insert close together within the propagating environment.

In many cases, the leaf surface can be reduced by cutting the leaves in half. However, trimming the leaves in this way puts extra stress on the broadleaved cuttings. Some such cuts may bleed slightly, making the cuttings wet to handle while they are being prepared and inserted. Fortunately the problem is only short-lived, and cut surfaces dry within a few hours. Dip each cutting base in rooting hormone and insert it into a pot of cuttings compost. Water the cuttings, and cover with a plastic bag to reduce water loss.

1 *Trim the leaves by gathering them together and cutting them across, with secateurs, about half way down each of the leaves.*

2 *Dip the base of each cutting into hormone rooting powder and shake off any excess. Insert the cuttings into cuttings compost.*

Hardwood cuttings

Hardwood cuttings can be taken at any time in late autumn and winter, but those taken before the cutting is fully dormant, in late autumn, are likely to be the most successful. Because the soil is moist and relatively warm, they have a chance to produce small roots before the onset of winter and should start into stem growth by mid-spring.

Select a healthy shoot, 23-60cm (9-24in) long, from the current season's growth of the parent plant. Cut it straight across the bottom of the stem with sharp, pruning secateurs. Cut the tip at an angle (but if the buds are arranged opposite each other, as in buddleja, make a straight cut).

In a well-cultivated part of the garden, make a series of holes for the cuttings by

Planting cuttings
Press each cutting into the bottom of a hole formed by a fork.

pushing the tines of a garden fork up to 15cm (6in) into the soil. Insert one into each hole, so that it presses into the bottom. At least two-thirds of the cutting should be in the ground. Rake the soil around the cuttings and press it firmly around them. If conditions are dry, finish by watering the soil well. Then leave the hardwood cuttings to initiate roots. During the winter, a callus will form at the base of each cutting and it will start to produce roots. Retread around the cuttings after each hard frost. In spring, when the cuttings start to produce leaves, they are at their most vulnerable, so protect them carefully.

Where to cut a stem

Soft, immature stems are cut 6mm (¼in) below a leaf joint, or node, where the stem is harder and more resistant to fungal rots. Such a basal cut is called a nodal cut. Woodier, more mature stems are cut midway between the leaf joints. This cut, an internodal cut, is used less often than a nodal one. Use on plants, like vines, that can produce new roots anywhere on the stem, and those whose nodes are spaced far apart.

leaf node

leaf node

A nodal cut

leaf node

leaf node

An internodal cut

Improved rooting

To encourage a cutting to produce roots, the base of a stem can be 'wounded'. Make a shallow, angled, downward cut, 2.5cm (1in) from the base of the cutting so that a strip of bark is removed. This stimulates root production both from the base of the cutting and from the edges of the wound itself.

Another way to assist is to take a heel of bark from the parent branch, together with a cutting. This heel exposes the swollen base of the current season's growth, which has a great capacity for stimulating roots. It also gives the cutting a firm base, so it is well protected against rot.

Wounding a stem
Cut a wound near the stem base with a sharp knife. Keep your thumb tucked under the stem and move the knife blade and lower thumb together down the stem, making a shallow cut.

Heel cutting
Hold the shoot between finger and thumb and give it a short, sharp tug, both downwards and outwards, to tear it from the branch. Trim the bark and bruised tissue with a sharp knife.

Division

You can increase most perennials by splitting a clump of plants, complete with roots and growth buds, into small sections, each of which grows into a new plant, identical to the parent. Either plant the divisions straight into their new site, or into spare ground until they are ready to be planted out permanently. You can rejuvenate many perennials in this way every three to four years as the healthy, new outer sections, when replanted, produce vigorous plants. Division is best carried out when plants are semi-dormant and the soil is workable. Early spring is the main season, but some plants, such as bearded irises, should be left alone until after they have flowered.

How to divide roots

Plants with fleshy roots, such as hostas, need to be cut with a sharp knife into sections, ensuring that each has its own roots and growth buds. Carefully cut away and discard any old and rotten portions of the roots. Replant divisions immediately in well-prepared soil, and water them with a fungicidal solution to prevent them from rotting.

Plants with fibrous roots can be divided by easing the roots apart with your fingers or a knife. If the roots are too tough, you can split them into manageable sections with a garden fork. Replant immediately after division.

Dividing fleshy roots
1 *Wash the soil from the root mass so that healthy roots and new growth buds are clearly visible.*

2 *Use a sharp knife to split the plant into vigorous outer sections with their own roots and growth buds.*

Dividing fibrous roots
Insert two forks back to back in a clump and pull the two forks together to force the tines apart and split the clump into sections.

Runners

Some plants produce runners that develop new plantlets on contact with soil. Anchoring a tiny plantlet into a plunged pot will result in a new rooted plant in about six weeks.

Self-rooting plants
Sink a compost-filled pot under a plantlet and anchor it firmly with a wire hoop.

Root cuttings

Plants that produce shoot buds on their roots can be increased by taking root cuttings in late autumn and winter, while the plant is dormant. Put the cuttings outside in a cold frame. New shoots should emerge by mid-spring.

There are two methods for taking root cuttings. For plants with thick, fleshy roots, take cuttings about 7.5cm (3in) long and 2cm (¾in) thick. Cut the ends with a straight cut at the upper end and an angled cut at the root tip end (so that you work out which way up to plant them). Insert the cuttings into compost vertically with the straight tops level with the compost. Cover with 1.5cm (½in) of moist, sharp sand, then water with a fungicidal solution.

Thin, fibrous roots should be cut into sections 7.5cm (3in) long, with a straight cut. Place the cuttings horizontally on the compost and then cover with 1.5cm (½in) of moist, sharp sand, and water with a fungicidal solution.

1 *Lift the plant and remove complete sections of root.*

2 *Cut the end of the root nearest to the plant straight across.*

3 *Cut the thinner end, nearest to the root tip, with a sloping cut.*

4 *Insert cuttings so the straight end is level with the compost.*

5 *Cover with moist, sharp sand to stop the cuttings drying out.*

Layering

This is an ideal method of propagation for the new gardener because no great expertise or risk is involved. The young plant is separated from the parent plant only after it has formed roots and is growing independently. Layering especially suits woody plants and climbers, which are difficult to root from cuttings. The best times for layering are in early spring, before new growth begins, or in early summer as new growth is ripening.

Natural layering
Some shrubs with low branches, like Cotinus coggygria, *will layer themselves. Others can be persuaded by pegging down low branches.*

Simple layering

Select a vigorous, young, flexible shoot from the shrub or climber to be layered. At a point about 30cm (12in) back from the tip of the shoot make an angled cut on the underside, with a sharp knife. The cut should penetrate about a third of the way through the shoot. Twist the shoot to open the cut. Dig a shallow hole in the ground and half fill with good compost. Position the injured section of the shoot into the bottom of the hole, and secure it firmly with a wire peg, making sure the cut is left open. Replace the soil, firm it all down and water well with a fine spray. Do not let the area dry out. It may take a year or more for the shoot to root. Scrape the soil to check if there are roots and when they appear, sever the new plant from the parent plant and leave it for a further growing season before moving it to a new site.

1 *Choose a flexible, young stem that can be bent to touch the ground, and trim the side shoots.*

2 *Bend the stem to the ground and mark its layering position about 30cm (12in) from its tip.*

3 *Make an angled cut, with a knife, about a third of the way into the underside of the stem.*

4 *When the layered stem has rooted, which may take up to a year, sever it from the parent plant.*

Tip layering

Tip layering is the method used to propagate plants that produce long, flexible shoots capable of producing roots at the growing point (tip). Blackberry and other fruit bushes are often propagated in this way.

In early summer, choose one of the young, vigorous shoots and bend it over to touch the soil. Dig a hole, where it touches the ground, about 10cm (4in) deep, and bury the growing point of the shoot in it.

Firm the soil gently and water well. Over a period of six to eight weeks, this tip will first form roots and then produce a new shoot, which will emerge above the soil.

In autumn, sever the new plant from the parent plant by cutting just above a bud with sharp sectateurs. Then dig up the new plant and move it to its permanent site.

New plants from shoot tips
In early summer, dig a hole 10cm (4in) deep, bury the growing tip of a new-season shoot in it and firm in well. By autumn the tip will have rooted and a new plant developed. Sever the plant from its parent by cutting above a bud.

Plant problems

Always purchase strong, healthy, vigorous plants. Plants that do not appear true to type or have obvious signs of pests or disease should be rejected, because a sick plant can easily transfer disease to existing, healthy stock. Never use poor quality plants for the purposes of propagation, since weak cuttings rarely grow into sturdy, flourishing plants.

Choose the right plant for the right place, making sure that the soil pH, texture and type are compatible with the plant. Select an appropriate position to meet the plant's needs. For example, it makes sense to plant salt-tolerant subjects in coastal gardens.

Good preparation and correct planting are essential to promote the quick establishment of newly introduced plants, and to help keep them growing rapidly and strongly, especially during the first year. Plants that struggle to establish themselves are much more likely to succumb to disease. It is vital to check plants regularly, so that problems can be spotted and dealt with early on.

Companion planting
Marigolds are planted close to vegetables in this informal vegetable garden because they attract hover-flies, which feed on aphids.

Pest and disease controls

In a well-cultivated and carefully tended garden, with varied planting, there are unlikely to be many problems. However, when they do arise, gardeners must decide how to deal with pests and diseases.

Organic control

This is based on the use of natural methods to help plants resist, tolerate or recover from pest and disease attacks. In many respects, it is a move back to some of the traditional remedies for gardening problems – methods such as crop rotation. The main aspects of using organic methods of control include:

• **Resistance** Many newly introduced plants have a natural tolerance or resistance to pests and diseases.
• **Safety** Many natural chemicals are derived from plant extracts. They break

down quickly and do not persist in the soil, so they need to be applied regularly.
• **Hygiene** Clearing away plant and weed debris reduces potential breeding sites for pests and diseases. Good crop rotations can prevent the build-up of particular types.

Chemical control

Chemicals offer a quick and simple solution to many pest and disease problems. Many are very effective, but they are better used as a last resort for several reasons:
• **Safety** Many chemicals are toxic and can be harmful to humans, pets and wildlife. Apply with extreme care.
• **Residue** Traces of chemical may remain in the soil and plant tissue for long periods.
• **Tolerance** Many pests and diseases are able to adapt. They develop a resistance to chemicals which are used persistently for long periods.

Simple biological controls

To avoid depending on pesticides, combine methods like the earwig trap, below, with biological controls. An increasing number of pests and diseases can be controlled by a natural predator or parasite. Start early in the season, before pests proliferate. This method works best in an enclosed environment, such as a greenhouse. It is worth bearing the following factors in mind:
• **Safety** There is no need to use protective clothing or dispose of unused chemicals. Most of these natural predators are specific to a limited range of pests and cannot harm pets and wildlife.
• **Residue** These controls do not involve poisonous chemicals, so no poisonous traces remain in the soil or plant tissues.
• **Understanding** For this control to be effective, you

need some knowledge of the life-cycle of the pest or disease.
• **Adaptability** For the predator or parasite to survive and function, a small amount of the pest or disease must be left. This is a new objective – not to totally eliminate the pathogen, but to control it.

Earwig trap
To trap earwigs, fill a pot with straw and invert it on a pole.

How to recognize and control common pests

Aphids
Dense colonies of small pale-green, through pink to greeny-black, insects. Many species transmit viruses from one plant to another, often resulting in plant death.
Symptoms Distorted shoot tips and young leaves, sticky coating on lower leaves, often accompanied by a black, sooty mould.
Plants attacked A wide range of plants.
Prevention Remove and burn badly infected plants.
Control Spray at regular intervals as soon as the first aphids appear in late spring.

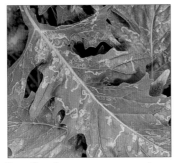

Leaf miners
Very small insect larvae that feed inside the plant leaves.
Symptoms Leaves of plants develop small, pale-green or white lines. These are the feeding tunnels of the insects. They are of nuisance value rather than causing serious damage.
Plants attacked Holly and chrysanthemums are among the many plants attacked.
Prevention Pull off and discard affected leaves as soon as they are spotted.
Control Spray dimethoate or malathion at regular intervals as soon as insects are seen.

Red spider mites
Minute mites that suck the sap of plants.
Symptoms Stunted growth. Yellow, curled and mottled leaves, covered with a fine webbing.
Plants attacked Many, but vines, carnations, cucumbers and chrysanthemums are particularly vulnerable.
Prevention Spray the undersides of leaves frequently with water, and maintain high humidity.
Control Spray with a systemic insecticide at regular intervals, or introduce the parasitic insect *Phytoseiulus*.

Vine weevil larvae
White, legless grubs with a black/brown head, usually curled into a 'C' shape. Feed on plant roots.
Symptoms Plants wilt or collapse. When examined, most of the roots are missing. Small semi-circular notches bitten out of leaf edges.
Plants attacked A wide range, including begonias, camellias, cyclamen, fuchsias, primulas and rhododendrons.
Prevention Keep soil clear of debris and litter which offer hiding places.
Control Treat soil with parasitic nematodes.

Earwigs
Fast-moving, small, shiny, brown insects, up to 2.5cm (1in) long, with a pincer-like gripper on the tail.
Symptoms Small, circular notches or holes in the leaves and flowers.
Plants attacked Herbaceous perennials, especially dahlias and chrysanthemums, house plants and young vegetables.
Prevention A small amount of damage may be acceptable as earwigs also eat quite a number of aphids.
Control Traps such as straw-filled pots can be used. Spray badly affected plants with HCH or malathion.

Scale insects
Insects resembling small, brown blisters on the stems and leaves of plants. They suck the plant's sap.
Symptoms Stunted growth and yellowing leaves, a sticky coating on lower leaves, often accompanied by a black, sooty mould.
Plants attacked Many trees, herbaceous perennials and greenhouse plants.
Prevention Place a layer of barrier glue around the stems of plants.
Control In mid summer introduce Metaphycus. Apply malathion spray in late spring and early summer.

Slugs and snails
Slugs are slimy with tubular bodies. Snails are very similar, but have a circular shell.
Symptoms Circular holes in plant tissue. Damaged seedlings are usually killed.
Plants attacked A wide range, including hostas, herbaceous perennials, seedlings and food crops.
Prevention Keep soil well-drained and weed-free. Apply gravel around plants as a barrier. Remove plant debris.
Control Apply aluminium sulphate in spring, or scatter slug pellets round the base of plants. Slug traps filled with stale beer are very effective.

Wireworms
Thin, yellow bodies, pointed at each end.
Symptoms Holes in roots and tubers of plants, often causing the above-ground parts to collapse. Attacked seedlings are usually killed.
Plants attacked A wide variety, including herbaceous perennials, bulbs and bedding plants, as well as young vegetable seedlings.
Prevention Avoid planting susceptible plants for up to three years on soil which has recently been grassland.
Control A granular insecticide incorporated into the top 5cm (2in) of soil.

How to recognize and treat common diseases

Botrytis
A fungus infecting flowers, leaves and stems.
Symptoms Discoloured, yellowing leaves, covered with a grey mould. The stem may rot at ground level, causing the plant to fall over.
Plants attacked Any, including roses, house plants, bulbs, lettuce, bedding plants and tomatoes.
Prevention Prune out affected sections, remove and burn badly infected plants, and maintain good air circulation.
Control Spray with thiophanate-methyl.

Downy mildew
A fungus infecting leaves and stems. Can overwinter in the soil or in plant debris.
Symptoms Discoloured, yellowing leaves, with white patches on the lower surface. Plants often die slowly in the autumn.
Plants attacked Vines, roses and many herbs.
Prevention Avoid over-crowding, use resistant cultivars. Remove and burn badly infected plants, and maintain good air circulation.
Control Spray with the chemical fungicide mancozeb.

Fireblight
A bacterial disease which moves on a film of water, invading plant's soft tissue.
Symptoms Flowers and young shoots become blackened and shrivelled, leaves wilt and turn brown, shoots die back and plants die.
Plants attacked Many members of the rose family; cotoneaster, crab apple, hawthorn, pyracantha, mountain ash and quince.
Prevention Grow as few susceptible plants as possible.
Control Burn plants with the above symptoms, or cut out affected areas.

Powdery mildew
A parasitic, fungal disease invading softer tissues inside the leaf.
Symptoms White, floury patches on young leaves, distorted shoots and premature leaf fall.
Plants attacked A wide range of plants, including roses, fruit trees, herbaceous perennials and vegetables.
Prevention In autumn, prune out infected stems.
Control Spray thiophanate-methyl on young leaves at the first signs of fungal infection. The fungus cannot penetrate old leaves.

Coral spot
A common fungus invading the dead wood of plants. May invade live tissue later.
Symptoms Individual branches wilt in summer; grey-brown staining may be found under the bark. In autumn, dead branches are covered in small, salmon-pink, blister-like marks.
Plants attacked A wide range of woody plants, including Japanese maples, magnolias and pyracantha.
Prevention Prune during summer. Do not leave old dead prunings around.
Control Remove and burn infected material quickly.

Silver leaf
A fungus entering woody tissue of members of the cherry family.
Symptoms Leaves adopt a silvery sheen. Branches die back until the whole plant eventually succumbs. As the tree dies, brownish-purple, spore-bearing, fungal brackets appear on branches.
Plants attacked Any relative of the cherry family that has just been pruned.
Prevention Prune during the summer.
Control Prune infected branches from healthy trees, remove and burn badly infected trees.

Damping off
A group of soil-borne fungi which invade and kill the host plants.
Symptoms Seedlings fail to sprout during germination, or keel over, rot and die soon after germination.
Plants attacked Very young seedlings (usually within five days of germinating).
Prevention Good plant care and hygiene. When raising young plants, use sterilized compost and containers. Use seed treated with an appropriate fungicide.
Control Drench infected seedlings and seed trays with a copper-based fungicide.

Mosaic virus
A very simple organism which lives inside the plant, and feeds from it.
Symptoms Yellowing, distorted leaves and poor, weak growth, stunted shoots and striped, misshapen flowers and fruits.
Plants attacked A wide range, including alpines, bedding, house plants, herbaceous perennials, soft fruit and vegetables.
Prevention Buy virus-free plants and control aphids. Do not grow plants in soils infested with eelworms.
Control Remove and burn infected plants immediately.

How to recognize and treat common disorders

Fasciation
Irregular growth which may be caused by bacterial attack or genetic mutation.
Symptoms Twisted or flattened growth, often appearing as many stems joined together and leaves grouped in clusters.
Plants attacked Almost any plant, but it is more noticeable on woody plants.
Prevention None. Some plants are grown for the decorative appearance of the distorted growth.
Control Prune out distorted growths by removing complete stems and shoots.

Frost damage
Temperatures of below 0°C (32°F) causing death or injury to affected plants.
Symptoms Blackening of soft, new growth. Leaves on woody plants, annuals and half-hardy plants blacken and die in a few days. Some vegetables develop split stems as a result.
Plants attacked Almost any plant can suffer frost damage if temperatures fall enough.
Prevention Use fleece, cold frames and cloches to protect young or small plants from sharp frosts.
Control None.

Nitrogen deficiency
Lack of available nitrogen affects plant growth.
Symptoms Pale-green leaves eventually turning yellow and pink, thin spindly stems, stunted growing tips.
Plants attacked Trees, fruit, shrubs, vegetables, herbaceous perennials, greenhouse and indoor plants.
Prevention Regular dressings of well-rotted manure and balanced, compound fertilizers.
Control In emergencies, apply sulphate of ammonia. For a long-term solution, add a high-nitrogen fertilizer.

Sun scorch
Damage caused by heat, due to direct sunlight on the surface of the plant.
Symptoms Dead, dry patches on tree bark. Hard, brittle leaves on greenhouse plants. Hard fruits with flaking skin.
Plants attacked Maples, beech, cherries and poplars; cyclamen and ferns; gooseberries, pears and tomatoes.
Prevention Shade plants, if possible. Protect larger trees by wrapping stems with hessian bandages. Keep greenhouses well ventilated.
Control See prevention.

Drought
Prolonged shortage of water.
Symptoms Plants wilt and collapse, dying within a short time. Leaves dry out and curl, often hanging dead on the plant for long periods.
Plants attacked All plants, but especially those grown in containers and young plants in light, sandy soils.
Prevention Regular dressings of well-rotted manure and organic matter. Mulch to reduce evaporation from the surface of the soil.
Control Water regularly and thoroughly, making sure that the soil is soaked, not just wet on the surface.

Lime-induced chlorosis
Growing plants in soil with too high an alkaline content for their particular needs.
Symptoms Stunted growth. Leaves turn yellow, starting between their veins. Affects older leaves first, and younger ones later.
Plants attacked Any plant, but acid-loving plants show symptoms first.
Prevention Maintain soil pH below 6.5, add peat and well-rotted manure regularly.
Control In the short-term, apply sequestered iron; longer-term, apply flowers of sulphur at 1kg to 10sq m (2lb to 10sq yds) of soil.

Phosphate deficiency
Lack of available phosphates affects plant growth.
Symptoms Reduced plant growth, leaves turn dull green then yellow. May worsen after periods of heavy rainfall.
Plants attacked Any plant, but those growing on clay or organic soils and seedlings are most susceptible.
Prevention Regular dressings of manure and balanced, compound fertilizers.
Control For a quick response, apply super-phosphate immediately. Bonemeal is good for slow, long-term release.

Waterlogging
Roots of plants suffer from a lack of oxygen.
Symptoms Yellowing leaves which often wilt despite having plenty of water. Bark flakes from woody plants. Badly affected specimens die back as their roots are killed.
Plants attacked Any, other than pond and bog plants.
Prevention Regular, deep cultivation and incorporation of organic matter to improve soil structure.
Control Install drainage pipes if the problem becomes severe. Grow plants on raised beds or ridges to overcome localized wet spots.

Pruning

Pruning is an important garden operation, which can significantly improve the look, health and flowering performance of many woody plants. Although it appears to be a complicated process, once you understand the basic principles and methods, you will find it interesting and rewarding to see the benefits it brings.

In its simplest form, pruning is a means of controlling plant growth, productivity and shape, by cutting and training. Sections of the plant are removed to encourage buds to develop lower down. This is essential when growing fruit, to ensure reliable cropping. In the case of ornamentals, rose pruning and hedge trimming are the most frequent operations.

Most trees and shrubs need little routine pruning. The process is performed more as a remedy – when a plant encroaches on a neighbouring plant or obstructs a path. Renovation pruning can improve a plant's appearance, but years of neglect or bad pruning cannot be rectified in one session. Some gardening styles require plants to be cut very precisely. In a parterre, plants are set out in geometric designs; in topiary, they are sculpted into shape.

Pollarded tree
Pollarding is a stylized form of pruning in which a tree is regularly cut back to the top of its trunk, to restrict size.

Pruning principles
The first stage of any pruning operation can be summarized in a rule we will call, 'The four Ds'. This means the removal of any dead, dying, diseased or damaged wood. Afterwards the remaining live, healthy growth can be assessed.

The second stage is to cut out any weak or straggly shoots, to give you a clearer idea of the framework that you have to work with. At this point, you will be able to decide which branches should be pruned back or removed to achieve well-balanced growth.

Remove unnecessary and badly placed growth, such as crossing or congested stems. The aim should always be to try to work with the natural growth habit of the plant. It is important to always retain the inherent grace of the tree, rather than impose an overzealous pruning regime which fights it.

Correct/incorrect pruning
A badly pruned tree (above) fails to reflect natural growth patterns and is prone to disease. A well-pruned tree (right), creates by contrast, a well-balanced healthy shape.

Reasons to prune

The five reasons to prune:
- To maintain plant health
- To obtain a balance between growth and flowering
- To train the plant
- To restrict growth
- To improve the quality of flowers, fruit, foliage or stems.

Plant health

You can eradicate pests and diseases by pruning out dead, damaged and diseased parts, but it is far more effective to prune as a preventative measure to maintain plant health. By thinning out the plant – removing congested growth and overcrowded stems – you allow plenty of light into the centre and encourage a good air flow. This will help to discourage pests and diseases. Prune out crossing stems as these rub against each other, causing damage which makes them more vulnerable to disease.

Balanced growth

Young plants channel their energy into producing vigorous growth rather than flowers. As the plant matures, the emphasis shifts – shoot production declines until little annual growth is added. Pruning encourages mature, woody plants to produce young wood – the source of their leaves and flowers.

Training

Pruning a young plant forms the framework of sturdy, evenly spaced branches which will eventually produce flowers and fruit. You can create a balanced, productive tree of the desired shape and size.

Restricting growth

Trees and shrubs left to develop naturally will grow larger and larger, which can be a problem in a restricted space. Pruning is necessary to keep plants within bounds.

Improving quality

A plant left unpruned will still produce flowers and fruit, but over time these become smaller. You can prune out older shoots and divert energy into the development of larger flowers and fruit.

Some deciduous shrubs, such as dogwood (*Cornus alba*), have brightly coloured bark and the best colour is produced on young stems. The most intense shades are produced by hard pruning.

Health
This shoot has died back due to bad pruning and must be cut back as far as healthy wood.

Training
Fruit tree stems are trained horizontally to encourage flowers and fruits to form.

Restricting growth
The trunk of a grafted tree must be kept clean of suckers as they deprive the top growth of vigour.

Quality
Removing dead flowers is vital to prevent seed formation and encourage further flowers to form.

Positioning pruning cuts

When pruning, it is extremely important not to harm or damage the plant in any way. To avoid this, you need to distinguish the different arrangements of buds on the stem and to make sure that the pruning cuts on a particular plant are positioned correctly.

For those plants where the buds are arranged alternately on the stem, you should make any pruning cut at an angle, 6mm (¼in) above an outward-facing bud. Any new growth will now grow away from the main stem. The bud itself should be just beneath the high point of the cut.

For those plants where the buds are arranged opposite to each other on the stem, you should make the pruning cut at a right-angle to the stem, just above a pair of buds and as close to the buds as possible, without damaging them.

The reason for cutting close to the buds is because the wound-healing capacity of the stem tissue is greater when close to a growth bud. If the cut is made too far away from it, the stem is more likely to die back to the bud, which not only looks unsightly, but may allow disease to take hold.

Alternate buds
On trees and shrubs where the buds or leaves are arranged alternately, make the pruning cut at an angle, diagonally across the stem, just above a bud or leaf that is outward facing.

Opposite buds
Where the buds and leaves are arranged opposite one another on the stem, make the pruning cut straight across. Cut as close to the buds as possible without causing them any damage.

Pruning trees

Trees give a sense of permanence and maturity to a garden. Once established, they do not need the regular attention that many shrubs require – but pruning can be used to control their shape and size, as well as to influence their vigour.

The method depends on the type and habit of the tree concerned. Flowering trees are pruned specifically to encourage flowers and fruit, others are pruned for their attractive foliage or colourful stems.

Evergreen trees
Many evergreens, like this magnolia, require little or no pruning. In this case, only deadheading of fading flowers is required.

Head formation

The top of a tree is called the head. The form can vary, depending on how the tree grows, has been grafted or is pruned. If the central leader is retained, the main stem of the tree goes right to the top.

To encourage branching, the end third of each lateral branch is removed. Branch-headed trees have the central leader removed so that an open centre develops, with similar-sized branches. To create a clear stem, lower branches are removed.

Central leader standard
The central leader is retained to form a feather shape.

Branch headed tree
The central leader is removed in order to develop an open centre.

Feathered tree
The natural form of many young trees, in particular conifers.

Weeping standard
Naturally weeping form grafted onto a clear-stemmed tree.

Training a new leader

If a tree loses its leading shoot by breakage, prune the damaged leader back to a healthy-looking bud. The shoot that develops from the bud

Competing leader
If two leaders are competing, cut out the weaker, more crooked shoots to leave a dominant one.

should be trained against a bamboo cane, so that it grows straight. Once the shoot becomes woody it will grow in the desired direction without need of support. If two leaders compete, prune out the weaker.

Supporting a leader
Train the shoot straight, against a bamboo cane, until it becomes woody.

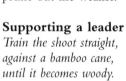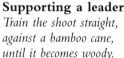

Water shoots
Excessively hard pruning may result in the trunk or branches of a tree producing masses of water (epicormic) shoots, especially around large wounds where branches have been removed. These shoots can then lead to congested growth, which will deprive the tree of its health and vigour.

They should be removed or thinned out as soon as they develop. You can then train one strong shoot as a replacement for the branch which has been taken away.

Removing water shoots from the base
A hooked pruning knife removes unwanted water shoots growing from the base of the tree.

Removing water shoots from a wound
Water shoots are often produced at the edge of old wounds where branches have been removed.

Suckers

Many trees propagated by grafting – artificially joining two separate plants together to form a single plant – may produce unwanted shoots or suckers from below the graft union, or from the roots.

These should be removed by pulling or cutting them from the tree before they become too large.

Grafted tree with sucker
This purple-leafed cherry (left) has a green-leafed sucker growing below the graft union. It must be removed before it becomes too large. Failure to do so will allow the green-leafed rootstock to predominate over the top growth.

Removing the sucker
Trace the sucker as far back as possible to its point of origin (right) and pull or cut it out.

Removing branches

When pruning larger, deciduous trees with well-developed branches, prune after leaf-fall. Care must be taken when removing branches. Do not remove a heavy branch by cutting it from above, flush with the trunk – the results can be disastrous. The branch will tear down into the trunk of the tree, causing a large, gaping wound which is a potential site for fungal infection. To avoid such a catastrophe, adopt safe pruning procedures. Cut the branch down gradually, section by section, to reduce the weight, before you reach the trunk of the tree.

1 *Make a cut, not too deep, on the underside of the branch, 30-45cm (12-18in) along from where it leaves the trunk.*

2 *Make the second cut on top of the branch, further out along the branch, 5-7.5cm (2-3in) away from the first cut.*

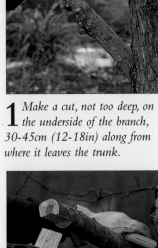

3 *When the second cut overlaps the first, the branch will snap along the grain and should fall clear without tearing.*

4 *Make a final cut parallel to the trunk to remove the remaining branch stub. Do not cut into the branch collar.*

Pruning deciduous trees

Deciduous trees are usually pruned when dormant, in late autumn or winter – but do not cut trees such as birch and maple at this time, or the sap will bleed. Prune these later on, in midsummer.

Young trees

Prune young trees to develop a balanced framework with a straight stem and well-spaced branches. Early pruning is important for trees with buds arranged in pairs, such as ash and maple, as, if the central stem is allowed to 'fork' into two, it may split.

During the first three years, prune ornamental trees, such as crab apples, to create a clear, vertical stem. Soon after planting, remove competing shoots and any thin or crossing shoots. In the first spring, prune off all lateral shoots from the bottom third of the tree and reduce all lateral shoots on the tree's middle third by half. In early winter, remove the reduced lateral shoots on the middle third. Repeat over the next two years until you have a clear stem of 1.8m (6ft).

Mature trees

Only prune established ornamental trees to maintain their shape and vigour. Thin any overcrowded, whippy branches in the centre of the head, to allow light and air into the centre of the tree. Any large branches which upset the overall balance and shape of the tree should be reduced in size, to prevent them from dominating the head of the tree. Excessive pruning of vigorous trees, when they are dormant, may result in quantities of long, sappy shoots. It may better to prune in the summer and avoid this eventuality.

Pruning evergreen trees

Conifers and broad-leaved evergreen trees are usually pruned in late spring.

Mature trees

Established, evergreen trees need little regular work. Pruning is usually a matter of removing dead, damaged or diseased branches, by cutting back to a strong, healthy shoot or removing the branch entirely. Cut out badly placed, weak or crossing laterals and remove competing leaders.

Never reduce the height of a conifer by cutting out the top, because this often leaves an ugly, mutilated shape. It is better to dig up the tree.

Young trees

You can establish a strong main stem or central leader by training a strong, vertical shoot upwards. Prune out any leaders that are competing with one another, as well as badly placed laterals or weak and crossing stems.

Pruning shrubs

There are several excellent garden shrubs that need only a light trim in the way of pruning. These include broad-leaved evergreens, such as some cotoneasters, ruscus and sarcococca. However, most shrubs, if left to grow unpruned, gradually deteriorate. Regular pruning enables them to grow and flower well, over a long period, and may even extend their life. Flowering shrubs are usually pruned very soon after the flowers have died away but, inevitably, there are exceptions. *Buddleja davidii* varieties flower in late summer but are not pruned until the following spring, to avoid frost damage to the new growth. The real dilemma comes with shrubs grown for their ornamental fruits, because they cannot be pruned after flowering, or the fruits will be sacrificed as a result. These plants are usually left until the main display of fruit has finished before they can finally be pruned.

Mixed shrub border
The beauty of ornamental flowering shrubs, such as the weigela and viburnum shown here, is enhanced by careful, well-timed pruning.

When to prune

Prune most established ornamental shrubs according to their flowering habit. The majority will produce flowers from a particular shoot only once. This may be a one-year-old shoot, in the case of forsythia, or a two-year-old shoot for kolkwitzia. Shrubs can be divided into four basic pruning groups (see below).

Other significant factors to take into account are the shrub's ability to produce replacement growth and the age of flower-bearing stems. The golden rule is to prune after flowering those shoots which have just flowered.

With all pruning groups, start by removing dead branches and trimming diseased or damaged shoots back to healthy tissue. On variegated shrubs, growth that has reverted to plain green must be pruned out. Then carry out any pruning for shape, or for fruit or flower formation, as usual.

Group 1
Requires very little or no pruning. Includes:

Amelanchier
Buddleja globosa
Camellia
Chimonanthus
Daphne
Elaeagnus pungens
Hamamelis
Magnolia stellata
Osmanthus
Viburnum tomentosum

Group 2
Flowers on the current season's growth; pruned in spring. Includes:

Buddleja davidii
Euonynus europaeus cvs
Forsythia
Fuchsia magellanica
Hibiscus
Hydrangea
Lavatera
Lavandula
Phygelis
Spiraea japonica

Group 3
Flowers on previous season's growth; pruned in summer after flowering. Includes:

Buddleja alternifolia
Chaenomeles
Deutzia
Exochorda
Kolkwitzia
Philadelphus
Rhododendron liteum
Ribes sanguineum
Spiraea arguta
Weigela

Group 4
Has a suckering habit or coloured stems. Includes:

Berberis
Corylus
Fuchsia
Hypericum patulum
Mahonia aquifolium
Rhus
Rosa nitida
Rosa rugosa
Sarcococca
Spiraea x *billiardii*

Daphne bholua 'Gurkha'

Hibiscus syriacus 'Blue Bird'

Weigela 'Florida Variegata'

Berberis x stenophylla

Pruning deciduous shrubs

Before starting to prune any shrub, always look at the habit and growth pattern of the plant. This provides clues to its pruning requirements.

The flowering pattern of mop-head hydrangeas puts them in the category of shrubs that flower on the previous season's wood. Such Group 3 plants should be pruned after flowering – but these hydrangeas are an exception. They flower in late summer and autumn, but the buds are prone to frost damage in the winter. Because of this, rather than pruning soon after flowering, the dead flowers are left on the plant over winter to protect the buds. The shrub is then pruned in late spring.

Young shrubs

Deciduous shrubs are more likely to need formative pruning than evergreens. This is best done in the dormant season, between mid autumn and mid spring, at planting time or soon after.

Cut back crossing branches to one-third of their length, positioning the cut so that the topmost bud faces outwards. This directs growth away from the centre of the plant. Cut out weak and congested shoots, and cut back unbalanced shoots to a suitable outward-facing bud or prune them out altogether.

As a general guide, if an over-vigorous shoot is distorting the framework of the plant, cut it back lightly rather than severely. If there is no balanced framework of branches, cut the plant back hard to promote strong, new shoots. Hard pruning of a vigorous shoot can stimulate even stronger growth – a principle summed up in the adage, 'Prune weak growth hard, but prune strong growth only lightly'. Try to bear this in mind when correcting the appearance of any misshapen shrub.

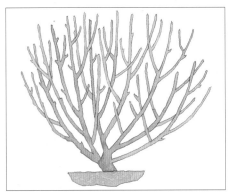

Congested stems
Remove up to one-third of the stems from a congested plant. This encourages a good air flow and discourages pests and diseases.

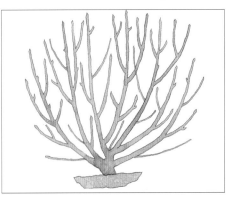

Weak stems
Cut out any thin, weak or spindly stems which are a drain on the plant's resources and are more vulnerable to pests and diseases.

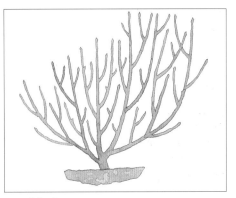

Lopsided stems
Over-vigorous shoots that distort the framework of the plant should be cut back lightly. Pruning too hard stimulates growth.

Pruning shrub and species roses

This is a large and varied group of roses. All of the species and most of the shrub roses, both old and modern, flower on wood that is two years old, or older.

Many flower freely for a number of years without any formal pruning, other than dead-heading old flowers. When they are pruned, remove all weak, damaged, dead and diseased wood. Follow this by a light pruning, leaving as much flower-bearing wood as possible. For the repeat-flowering roses, this is particularly important. The best approach is to remove, completely, two or three of the oldest stems each year, so that over three or four years, all the growth is gradually renewed.

The best time for this method of pruning is immediately after flowering, because this gives the plant the chance to channel its energy into developing new stems. The main exceptions are species, such as *Rosa rugosa*, *Rosa moyesii* and their hybrids, which are valued for their attractive display of hips in autumn and winter. Pruning of these species should be left until late winter.

Standard rose – before
Hard pruning can be used to stimulate vigorous new growth.

Well-pruned standard rose
After pruning, the standard rose has a balanced framework of shoots.

Bush rose – before
Any thin, weak and inward-pointing shoots must be cut out.

Well-pruned bush rose
After pruning, only strong, healthy shoots remain.

Mature deciduous shrubs

The routine maintenance of deciduous shrubs involves the removal of any dead, diseased or damaged wood. This work can be done throughout the year and you should act promptly as soon as you spot any of these problems.

With any shrub which needs to be pruned, it is advisable to remove two or three old stems by cutting them down to ground level. This stimulates new growth, keeps the centre of the plant open and helps air to flow through it, keeping down pests and diseases. Pruning for flowering depends on when the plant's flowering occurs.

Group 1
These plants hardly ever need pruning: most daphne species and hybrids seem to resent pruning and do far better if they are left alone. See below for plants from the other pruning groups.

Group 2
Shrubs in this group flower on the current season's growth and are pruned in spring. Forsythia is simple to prune, as the dead flowers remain on the plant for some time. Remove the old flowering shoots. Cutting them out gives new growth the maximum time to develop and produce next year's flowers. If too many shoots are produced, thin them out in early spring to produce fewer, but larger flowers. If pruning when the flowers have fallen, the stem colour shows which are the older shoots. New growth is dull green, maturing to golden-brown; older stems are a faded, browny-grey and are thicker than younger ones.

Removing stems
Cut out surplus shoots in early spring to produce better flowers.

Pruning after flowering
Prune directly after flowering, when the dead flowers are visible.

Group 3
Summer-flowering plants, such as deutzia, produce flowers on new shoots which formed in the previous growing season. Many of these main shoots will originate from the base of the plant and produce flowers on short, lateral branches. This gives the shrub a tangled, twiggy appearance and it is best to remove about one-third of the stems every year. This pruning is best carried out as the flowers fade, with the oldest, thickest stems being removed close to ground level. A late spring frost occasionally kills the shoot tips of new growth – some tip pruning may be necessary early in the season, to remove the damaged parts.

Thinning out
Remove old flowering stems to encourage next year's flowers.

Reshaping
Cut out the oldest stems at ground level.

Group 4
Shrubs such as kerria, which are grown for their flowers as well as the bright-green colour of their stems, flower on the previous year's wood. Most of the new growth, however, originates from ground level.

Because these shrubs have a suckering habit, it is a good idea to prune out all the old, flowering shoots as close to soil level as possible, as soon as the flowering season has finished. By removing all these old stems, you will stimulate more flowers to grow in future years. It will also encourage the development of new, green stems which show the brightest colour through the winter months, giving you the added bonus of stem colour in the garden.

Cutting out old stems
Cut old stems almost to the base just after flowering, as they will not produce any more flowers.

Removing weak stems
Cut thin, weak stems at soil level as they rarely produce flowers and are prone to pests and disease.

Pruning for colourful stems and leaves
Some shrubs, such as certain dogwoods (*Cornus*), are grown for their colourful stems in winter, and others, such as golden elder, have attractive young foliage. Both are pruned severely to provide plenty of young growth, which has the best colour. Prune dogwoods annually or biennially, depending on their vigour. Cut out all weak shoots and hard prune the previous year's shoots of dogwood in early spring, cutting back stems to a few centimetres above ground. Hard prune golden elder in late winter, to a few centimetres high.

Hard pruning of old stems
In early spring, cut stems to just above ground level.

New stem growth
The red stems of dogwood provide rich colour in winter.

Pruning evergreen shrubs

The pruning method for most evergreen shrubs will depend upon the growth rate and the size of the plant when it reaches its ultimate height. However, regardless of size, there are some rules that apply to all such plants.

General principles

Generally speaking, evergreen shrubs need very little formative pruning. However, excessively vigorous growth will have to be corrected, as it can result in the plant growing into a lop-sided, unbalanced shape.

When evergreen shrubs need pruning, do it lightly in mid spring to reduce the risk of frost damage on the fresh pruning cuts. Cut back any vigorous shoots, by at least a third, to prevent the plants losing their shape, but do not prune too hard, as this results in even more vigorous growth. Remove thin, weak or straggly stems growing in the centre of the plant. Thin out overcrowded shoots, as they can become damaged by rubbing together. When establishing flowering plants, such as rhododendrons, take off flowering shoots before they fully develop in spring.

Repeat this pruning regime for the first two or three years after planting, until the shrub starts to take on the desired shape.

If plants show signs of dieback following a hard winter, especially at the shoot tips, they should be cut back to live growth after the risk of hard frost has passed.

Some smaller shrubs, such as lavender, have a naturally compact habit and only need dead-heading after the flowers have died. Trim back the long flower stalks, with Always begin by pruning out any dead, damaged and diseased wood. Cut it back to a point where the shrub has started to regrow, or where healthy tissue can be seen. To shears or secateurs, close to their base. Trim the shoot tips, too.

Many hybrid mahonias have a tall, upright habit with a large expanse of bare stem below the leaves. In spring, immediately after flowering, cut back the old, flower-bearing stems to form a strong framework of branches about 45cm (18in) above soil level. This encourages a branching habit, with flowers at a more manageable height.

judge whether branches are live, lightly scrape away some of the bark with a sharp knife or secateurs. A green layer indicates live tissue, brown indicates dead wood.

Pruning for shape
Remove any long, straggly shoots as they develop, before they spoil the shape and balance of the plant.

Pruning after flowering
After flowering, cut back the long, bare sections of stem to a cluster of leaves. This encourages new shoots to develop.

Light clipping
Cut dead flower stalks in spring and trim 2.5cm (1in) off the top growth to encourage branching. Do not cut into old wood.

Reversion

Many plant species have varieties with gold- or silver-variegated leaves. These brightly coloured varieties may revert to type and begin to produce shoots with plain, green leaves. Such shoots need to be removed immediately. Cut the reverted shoot back to the first variegated leaf – or, if necessary, remove the shoot completely. Varieties of plants with finely cut leaves may also revert to type and begin to develop coarser leaves. These should be treated in exactly the same way.

Removing green leaves
If a plant with variegated leaves produces a shoot that has reverted to green leaves, you must cut the shoot to the first variegated leaf, or remove the shoot completely.

Renovation

Old, neglected or untidy plants may respond to severe pruning and produce young growth from the base. First, decide whether the shrub is worth trying to renovate. Would it be wiser to dig it up and replant a new one?

To renovate, cut evergreen shrubs down to about 45cm (18in) in mid-spring, just before new growth starts. The following spring, cut back any strong, vigorous shoots which may affect the plant's overall balance. Cut out any weak or crossing shoots. In subsequent years, cut out thin, straggly shoots and shape the plant so that you restrict its growth.

Pruning for renovation
Cut old, untidy shrubs, such as this elaeagnus, down to about 45cm (18in) in mid-spring.

Pruning climbers and wall shrubs

It is important to bear the growth habit of the plant in mind when pruning climbers and wall shrubs, for this should influence your method of pruning and training. Climbers can be divided into groups, based on the way that they hold themselves. The different categories – clinging, scrambling, and twining plants – are illustrated below. Apart from self-clinging plants, such as ivy, climbing plants need some means of support, and these can range from free-standing arches and pergolas to wall mounts like trellis, netting or vine eyes and wire. Climbers can grow vigorously and become very heavy (see p. 90), so support them accordingly. Plant display is always enhanced by proper pruning. Careful training and tying-in, from a young age, are essential.

Vertical gardening
Providing suitable supports, along with careful pruning and training from an early age, ensures the best display from climbing plants.

Types of climber

Climbing plants can be divided up into four basic groups, as follows:
Clinging plants (such as common ivy). These plants attach themselves to surfaces by clinging with **aerial roots** or **sucker pads** and usually need no additional support.
Twining plants. This is a large group, including honeysuckle, clematis and wisteria. Parts of the plant twine themselves around a support – these parts may be **tendrils**, **leaf-stalks** or **stems**. A support system is usually required for twining plants.
Scrambling plants (such as roses). These have rapidly-growing stems, which grow through other plants, using **hooked thorns**. Scrambling plants must be tied to a support system.
Wall shrubs. These are not true climbing plants, but shrubs that are made to grow against a wall or fence. They usually need careful training to grow them against the vertical surface.

Aerial roots
Climbing hydrangea uses aerial roots to cling on to surfaces. Another plant in this category is Campsis *(trumpet vine).*

Sucker pads
Virginia creeper is unusual in that it is the only plant that attaches itself to surfaces and climbs using sucker pads.

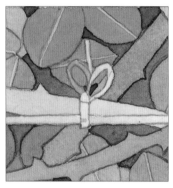

Hooked thorns
Scrambling roses climb using hooked thorns. Another plant in this category is Rubus.

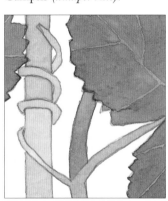

Twining tendrils
Grape vine climbs using tendrils. Other plants in this category include Ampelopsis *and* Passiflora.

Twining leaf stalks
Clematis climbs using twining leaf stalks. Eccremocarpus scaber and Tropaeolum speciosum are also in this group.

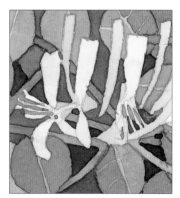

Twining stems
Honeysuckle climbs using its twining stems. Other plants in this category include Akebia quinata and Wisteria.

Pruning clingers

These climbing plants attach themselves to a wall or fence by means of sucker pads or aerial roots. They do not require a support system.

Evergreen plants such as ivy help to keep buildings cooler in summer and provide some insulation in the winter. However, when established, climbers with aerial roots can be over-vigorous. They create a problem on the walls and roofs of older houses and can do considerable structural damage. The roots grow into the lime-based mortar, and plant stems thicken, forcing guttering away. It is essential to check the climber's progress and prune the plant back hard, if necessary.

Young plants

Soon after planting, start by cutting the plant's growth back by half. As new extension growth begins, place and tie in the strongest stems, to achieve a well-spaced, balanced framework

Pruning (young campsis)
Cut back the stems to ground level. This will encourage new shoots to develop from the base.

of shoots. Coax them in the right direction, while still soft and pliable, with masonry nails or cable ties. In the second spring, cut back all of the sideshoots to a bud near the main stem. Strong stems will grow from these shoots during the season, forming

Training (a hydrangea)
Tie in shoots as they develop on a one-year-old natural clinger to give the plant a balanced framework.

the plant's framework. Cut back the tip of each stem the following year, to make the shoots branch and cover the wall, extending the main framework. Tie in the stems or help them grip. Cut back any other shoots to within two buds of the nearest stem.

Second-year growth
During the plant's second year, strong shoots develop, with aerial roots to help them grip.

Mature plants

Once plants with a clinging habit have become properly established, there is really very little regular pruning that you need do – apart, that is, from dead-heading to remove any spent flower heads from plants such as climbing hydrangea (*Hydrangea anomala* ssp. *petiolaris*).

The main time for pruning many of these climbers is in mid spring, just after the plants have started to develop new growth and the leaves are small. At this time of year, it is much easier to identify the stems that are dead,

damaged, diseased or weak and which need to be removed. If you leave it too long, they will be obscured by the fully developed leaves and young, new shoots.

Summer pruning will usually include essential maintenance, such as trimming vigorous growth from around doors and windows to prevent them being covered over. Aerial roots and sucker pads should be removed, carefully, from painted surfaces. Shoots that have worked their way under wooden cladding or roof tiles should be cut back with a sharp pair of secateurs.

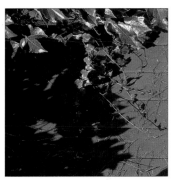

Before pruning
Vigorous clingers may need severe pruning to control them.

Pruning clingers
Prune out wayward shoots with a pair of sharp secateurs.

Renovation

Some climbers and wall shrubs cannot tolerate being cut down severely, and may not survive such harsh treatment. In such cases, it is advisable to carry out the renovation pruning in stages, over a two- or three-year period. Start by removing the oldest stems each year (usually the ones with the darkest coloured bark), so that over a couple of years all of the old growth is replaced by young, vigorous shoots.

The main disadvantage of renovating plants like this over several years is that the new growth that has been generated may become entangled with the old shoots which have yet to be removed, making it far more difficult to prune. To avoid this, cut down one side only of the plant in the first year.

Train the new shoots into the open spaces created by removing the unwanted growth. The remainder of the old stems are cut away in the second year and replacements trained and tied into the remaining space. It may take a further two years, or possibly even more, before the new growth is mature enough to produce flowers of its own.

Before hard pruning
This chaenomeles needs its shoots to be cut by half, back to ground level, to increase vigour.

Retraining after pruning
After hard pruning, remaining shoots are trained and tied in to create a fan shape.

Pruning twining climbers

Many twining climbers become very vigorous once established and if they are not regularly pruned, the plant will rapidly choke itself or form an unattractive, tangled ball of shoots. To succeed with this type of plant, make sure that new shoots are produced each spring. To do so, prune to stimulate new shoots and feed the plant in springtime. As the new shoots grow quickly, many of the flowers develop too high up on the plant to be fully appreciated. This problem is worse if the climber is not pruned and new shoots form above those from the previous year. Prune twining climbers regularly, unless they are grown to cover a large surface.

The twining habit leads to self-inflicted damage – stems wrap around each other, and some are crushed and split. Pests and diseases can become established in the wounds. Older stems need to be removed in rotation, and replaced by newer ones.

Young plants

In spring, or soon after planting, prune the new plant severely. Cut the thickest stems down to the lowest pair of strong, healthy growth buds and cut out thin, weak shoots completely. As the new growth begins, adjust its position. If necessary, tie the strongest stems to the support system to achieve a well-spaced, balanced framework of shoots. Until plants mature and start to cling by themselves, they may need to be tied at 30-45cm (12-18in) intervals to prevent wind damage to new shoots. Woody stems that develop while the shoots are maturing cannot be bent into the required position without inflicting damage.

The plant will be established by the second spring. Cut back all the sideshoots to a pair of buds close to the main stem, and tie in any loose shoots to the support system. A number of strong stems will grow from these shoots during the following season, forming the framework of the plant.

First year pruning
Cut back new plants (of honeysuckle here) in spring to the lowest pair of strong and healthy buds.

Second year pruning
Once the plant is well established, cut back all sideshoots to a pair of strong buds close to the main stem.

Tying in
As new shoots grow, train your plants (in this case clematis) by tying the strongest stems into position on their supports with soft twine

Mature plants

For most twining climbers, once a balanced framework of branches has been established, routine pruning consists of cutting back the lateral branches (side shoots) to a pair of buds close to the main stem.

For many plants, this pruning and training can be carried out through the autumn and winter. Tying in growth at this time will also help to prevent any loose stems being damaged by harsh winds.

Any damaged or dead shoots should be removed completely. To encourage flowering, one of the oldest stems is often cut back and a younger replacement tied into position. Neglected, climbing honeysuckles, in particular, may develop tangled stems that bear foliage and flowers at the the tops of shoots only. To correct the problem, prune hard in early to mid-spring, so that new shoots can develop and then be trained in. If children have access to your garden, always prune honeysuckle immediately after flowering too – the berries are attractive but highly poisonous.

Tying in
Spread out the new shoots and tie in position.

Frost damage
Cut out any frost-damaged shoots, back to healthy growth.

Renovation pruning
Shoots are cut back hard to the main stem for a better display.

Pruning wisteria

Wisteria flowers are formed on short spurs, mostly found on branches which are trained horizontally. Prune mature plants twice a year. In summer, tie shoots to be used as part of the framework into a horizontal position. Cut back new, long, lateral shoots, growing at right angles, to 15–20cm (6–8in) from the main stem. In late winter, cut back summer-pruned shoots to form spurs of two to three strong buds. (These will carry the flowers). Cut back to 15–20cm (6–8in), or remove, secondary growths formed after the summer pruning.

Pruning long shoots
Wisteria is extremely vigorous. To prevent sections of the stem being bare, the long shoots will need to be cut back in summer.

1 *In summer, after flowering, cut back new growth to 15cm (6in) to control vigour and promote flower buds.*

2 *In late winter, cut back the summer-pruned shoots to 3-4 buds. Also cut back any secondary shoots formed after the summer pruning to 15cm (6in).*

Pruning clematis

Clematis have the longest flowering period of any group of climbers. During most months of the year, some clematis or other is producing flowers. Prune as for twining climbers, but make sure you know when the clematis flowers, as the key to pruning is the flowering season.

Group 1 Early flowering species. Flowers from January through to late May.
Clematis alpina and cvs
Clematis armandii and cvs
Clematis cirrhosa and cvs
Clematis macropetala and cvs
Clematis montana and cvs

Many of the clematis in this group require little routine pruning. When necessary, the best time to prune is straight after flowering. This allows time for new growth to develop, so that the plant will flower the following spring.

Group 2 Early, large-flowered cultivars. Flowers from early June to early July.
Clematis 'Barbara Jackman'
Clematis 'Carnaby'
Clematis 'Daniel Deronda'
Clematis 'Duchess of Edinburgh'
Clematis 'Elsa Späth'
Clematis 'General Sikorski'
Clematis 'Henryi'
Clematis 'Lasurstern'

Clematis 'Marie Boisselot'
Clematis 'Mrs N. Thompson'
Clematis 'Nelly Moser'
Clematis 'Niobe'
Clematis 'The President'
Clematis 'Vyvyan Pennell'
The flowers are produced on stems up to 60cm (2ft) long, formed during the previous season. Any pruning should be done in early spring. Remove any dead, weak, or damaged growth. Cut back healthy stems to just above a strong pair of leaf buds.

Group 3 Late-flowering species and cultivars. Flowers from early July through to October.
Clematis florida and cvs

Clematis tangutica and cvs
Clematis viticella and cvs
Clematis 'Comtesse de Bouchaud'
Clematis 'Duchess of Albany'
Clematis 'Ernest Markham'
Clematis 'Gipsy Queen'
Clematis 'Hagley Hybrid'
Clematis 'Jackmanii'
Clematis 'Lady Betty Balfour'
Clematis 'Perle d'Azur'
Clematis 'Ville de Lyon',
Plants in this group produce flowers on stems of the current season's growth.

Pruning involves removing the previous season's growth by cutting plants down to a strong pair of buds to within 45cm (18in) of soil level in spring.

C. macropetala **'Jan Lindmark'**

C. **'Nelly Moser'**

C. viticella **'Mme Julia Correvon'**

Pruning scrambling climbers

The scrambling climbers have rapidly growing stems, which clamber through other plants in the wild. They use hooked thorns and a rapid extension of lax, vigorous shoots to attach themselves to, and gain support from, nearby plants and structures.

Scrambling climbers are capable of growing through other plants unaided, but if the intention is to grow them on a vertical structure like a wall or fence, a support system is needed. The plants will need to be tied to the support system and a constant programme of tying and training will need to be maintained to keep the plant growing in the desired direction.

Many scrambling climbers have a tendency to produce most of their flowers on the upper third of the plant, especially when grown up a vertical support. A useful tip is to train the growth at an angle of 45 degrees around the vertical support; this will promote the production of more flowers lower down the plant, providing a more impressive display.

Climbing roses
Rosa 'Madame Caroline Testout, Climbing' is a vigorous climbing 'sport' that has graced walls and fences since 1901.

Young plants

Plants such as climbing roses are not true climbers. They must be trained to go in the required direction, and tied to a support. Apart from removing dead, diseased, damaged or weak growth, they should not be pruned in the first year after planting, and, possibly, not in the second year, unless they have made exceptional growth. When the new shoots become long enough to tie in, begin training the plants.

As with most flowering climbers, the shoots should be trained horizontally, by tying them to supports to encourage flowering. Keep the shoots evenly spaced and tied into position. Cut back all sideshoots to within 7.5cm (3in) of a vigorous shoot.

If these scrambling plants are not carefully trained, they will grow into a tangle of unwieldy and unhealthy shoots. This results in poor air circulation and encourages the incidence of fungal diseases, such as black spot, mildew and rust. Dense, bushy growth also makes it very difficult to control diseases and pests.

Tying in stems
Tying and training of young shoots needs to be done on a regular basis, to keep the plant growing in the desired direction.

Neatening up
Trimming away any surplus string after tying is a cosmetic measure to help to give the plants a natural-looking appearance.

Mature plants

Many scrambling plants flower profusely for years without any other treatment than general pruning – the removal of weak or damaged shoots and congested growth in autumn.

Leave the strong, main shoots unpruned, unless they are exceeding their allotted space, in which case, shorten them by cutting them back to a strong, new shoot. Otherwise, simply shorten the sideshoots to within 7.5cm (3in) of a vigorous shoot. Make sure you train all the new season's growth to the supports, while they are still flexible, to establish a well-balanced framework and prevent wind damage.

If the base of a scrambling climber becomes very bare, renewal pruning may be necessary. Cut 25–30 per cent of the oldest shoots to within 15cm (6in) of ground level. This encourages the growth of vigorous, new shoots.

Shortening stems
Flowered stems should be reduced by about two-thirds, to an outward-facing bud.

Removing weak stems
To achieve a healthy, well-shaped plant, remove weak stems by cutting them back to the base.

Pruning wall shrubs

There are a great number of shrubs and a few small trees which can be trained against a wall or fence, and this can greatly increase the range of plants which can be grown in the garden.

For those shrubs that are slightly tender and need a degree of winter protection, a wall or fence can provide the shelter required. In order to manipulate a plant to grow in a flat vertical plane, the shoots and branches must be pruned and trained to cover the support with a framework of evenly distributed stems and branches. This is often difficult as the plant's natural tendency is to grow into the brightest light, which means the shoots will grow away from the support.

To control this natural tendency, pruning and training are combined to direct the growth into the desired directions. In order to achieve the right effect, the plant's natural habit and growth pattern has to be taken into account, and any pruning should be very specific to the plants individual needs.

A sheltered site
Tender shrubs such as this ceanothus, *a plant originating from California, benefit from being planted against a sunny wall.*

Young plants

Prune young wall shrubs immediately after planting. Cut out any damaged or diseased shoots and remove any thin, spindly stems. Train plants during the first growing season. Position and tie in the strongest stems to the support system to achieve a well-balanced framework of shoots, usually in a fan shape. Do this as the shoots develop, as later they become woody and may be damaged if bent into position. Carry out formative pruning in spring, after the risk of frost is past.

Tying in stems
Tie young, pliable shoots into a fan shape on the wall, before they become too woody to be manipulated easily.

Pruning for shape
Prune any shoots that are growing directly away from the wall, so that you maintain it as a well-shaped wall shrub.

Removing dead stems
Prune out any dead leaves and stems to improve appearance and remove potential sites where pests and diseases can get a hold.

Mature plants

For routine pruning, remove dead or damaged wood to prevent infection spreading, and cut back any weak shoots. Straggly branches, or those growing out at right-angles to the wall, should be removed. Tie in any long shoots which are to be kept as part of the plant's framework. As new growths are tied in, check existing ties to make sure plant stems are not being damaged or restricted by them. As a rule, prune wall shrubs that flower on last year's growth after the plants have flowered, and shrubs that flower on the current season's growth in spring.

New growth of pyracantha appears in summer after flowering and may hide the berries. To avoid this, prune mature plants in mid summer, cutting shoots to within 10cm (4in) of the main stem. These shoots will then form spurs to carry next year's crop of flowers.

Pruning for shape
Saw off any outward-growing branches for neatness.

Pruning after flowering
Cut older spurs to within 10cm (4in) of main stem after flowering.

Pruning hedges

Hedge clipping is, simply, pruning done in certain way to achieve a particular purpose, such as to form a shelter belt. The same general principles apply, but the method depends on the result required.

Formal hedges demand regular clipping or trimming to form a dense mass of compact shoots. Informal hedges take less work to achieve the desired effect. The timing and method is mainly determined by the flowering time but, as a rule, remove old flower-bearing branches as soon after flowering as you can. Plants producing berries should not be pruned until after the fruits have finished.

Tapestry hedges are made up of a mixture of plants, such as beech alternating with yew or holly. Mixing deciduous and evergreen species provides a colourful background, but use plants with similar growth rates.

Flowering hedge
A mature and well-tended Rosa 'Frühlingsmorgen' makes a very exuberant, informal hedge at the height of its flowering season

Young hedges

The success of a hedge depends on its treatment during the first two or three years. Formative pruning produces even growth over the entire surface, as well as controlling the height.

Immediately after planting, cut back a new hedge to between one- and two-thirds of its original height. Cut back any strong, lateral branches, by about half, to encourage the plants to establish more rapidly and form a dense, bushy habit from ground level. Repeat this process in the second year by severely pruning the sides and top of the hedge. Most of the extension growth forms along the hedge line between the plants, forcing them to grow into one another.

The severity of this initial pruning depends on the type of plant. The aim is to encourage plenty of bottom growth, or the base may remain relatively bare while the upper hedge is dense. If the formative pruning is done well and the new growth trimmed back by half, at least twice each year, a dense, narrow hedge is formed, about 75cm (2½ft) wide at the base, which is ideal for most situations.

Training young hedges
The speed of growth of any hedge depends on the plants used for it, as does its eventual thickness. Some plants are better suited to barrier hedging, others to ornamental screening. It will take four to five years for a deciduous hornbeam hedge to form any kind of protective barrier; an evergreen privet will take three to four, while yew will take up to 10 years but all plants, no matter what their speed of growth, must be pruned back hard in the early years or they will fail to bush out and create the impenetrable screen required.

Broad-leaved evergreen hedges
Pruning broad-leaved evergreens with shears mutilates many larger leaves and spoils the overall effect of the hedge. Leaves cut in half slowly turn yellow and die, and are very prone to attack by pests and diseases.

Use secateurs to prune back new growth. This also helps to reduce the number of damaged stems or branches. Remove any diseased parts quickly.

Stopping a leader
Cut back the main stem to encourage side shoots to grow.

Trimming laterals
Cut back any laterals by about half to encourage a bushy habit.

Formative pruning
Hard prune when mature to ensure even, vigorous growth.

Removing shoots
Prune back broad-leaved evergreen hedges by removing the tips of growing shoots with secateurs.

Mature formal hedges

As the hedge becomes taller, trim the sides to a sloping angle so that the top of the hedge is only about a third as wide as the base, or about 25cm (10in) wide. When the hedge has reached its intended height, a frame or template can be made of the hedge profile, and this can be used as a quick guide, when trimming, to keep the hedge to an even, uniform shape.

Formal hedges should always be shaped to be narrower at the top than at the base. This exposes all parts of the hedge to the light, stops parts of it dying out, (especially at the base) and makes trimming easier. This sloping angle helps the hedge to resist strong winds and to shed snow, rather than have it accumulate on the top, causing damage. This is a particular problem with evergreens, as they can collect large quantities of snow and ice in winter weather.

Trimming techniques

Start by trimming the sides of the hedge with shears or hedge trimmers. Work upwards from the base of the hedge so that the clippings fall out of the way as the work progresses. To make sure the top of the hedge is level, use a taut line set at the required height. It is wise to use a brightly coloured line, as this will reduce the chance of accidentally cutting through it. Clip the top of the hedge to the line, clearing clippings as you work.

Power hedge trimmer

These are ideal for long hedges which are to be trimmed to a formal shape on a regular basis. The electric ones have several advantages over the petrol-powered models. They are lighter, make far less noise and produce no fumes. When using a mechanical trimmer always keep the blade parallel to the surface of the hedge.

Using a trimmer
To protect yourself, wear gloves and goggles. Cut the hedge in a broad sweeping action, working from the bottom upwards.

Clipping sideshoots
Clip sideshoots to remove the growing tip of each shoot and encourage bushy growth.

Trimming to an A-shape
Trimming the hedge to be narrower at the top prevents snow settling and damaging it.

Cutting line
Use brightly coloured string stretched tautly to make sure that the hedge is cut in a straight line.

Renovating hedges

The method used can vary, but in extreme cases the plant is cut to within 10cm (4in) of the base to stimulate the production of new shoots. As the hedge regrows, the process of formative pruning and training will have to be carried out as for a newly-planted hedge.

Phased renovation pruning involves cutting the hedge back in stages so the effect is not so drastic. Cut one side back to the main stems in the first year and then repeat the procedure on the other side of the hedge the following year.

Such drastic action can create problems, such as a sudden lack of privacy, for instance. Or a previously sheltered area might suddenly become exposed, to adverse effect. Consider these risks when planning the operation. Most conifers do not have the ability to produce new growth from old wood and so are not really suited to renovation pruning.

Hard pruning a hedge
This promotes new growth from the base to the top of an old hedge.

Maintaining a healthy hedge

A hedge not only provides shelter for surrounding plants, but also for anything growing or living inside it. At certain times of year, the enclosed environment inside the hedge is warm and humid. These are the ideal conditions for colonization by pests and diseases – and for their spread. This makes pruning even more important.

Any dead or dying wood which is left in the hedge can, potentially, be the very first place where diseases establish themselves – so any infected wood must be removed as soon as it is spotted. For deciduous plants, this may be in the autumn when the leaves have fallen. For evergreen plants, the ideal time is when the hedge is being trimmed and there is less foliage to obscure any plant problems.

When dead wood is being removed, always cut back into live, healthy tissue, as this will reduce the chances of a secondary infection.

Removing diseased wood
Cut out any infected, dead or dying wood as soon as you see it.

Mature informal hedges

Informal flowering or mixed hedges are far less work than formal types, and only need pruning once a year. An informal hedge should be treated as a row of shrubs rather than the single entity of a formal hedge. The timing of pruning depends on the flowering season, as any cutting back is usually done after the flowers have died.

Prune a berrying hedge after the birds have eaten the berries. Remove the old stalks and shoot tips, which held the fruits, to make room for new flowers. Cut back a number of flower-bearing shoots close to ground level.

Mixed hedge before pruning
Mixed shrubs in a hedge will grow at different rates. Prune once a year when hedge starts to look untidy.

Mixed hedge after pruning
Cut back any very vigorous plants, removing long, struggling stems. Lightly clip the remainder.

Flowering hedge
Prune a flowering hedge after flowering. Cut shoots close to the ground to encourage new shoots to grow from the base.

Encouraging growth
Cut flower-bearing shoots to the ground after the flowers have died.

Suitable hedging plants

Plant	Evergreen/ deciduous	Planting distances m/ft	Formal/ Informal/ Either	Best height	When to prune or clip
Berberis thunbergii (Barbery)	Deciduous	90cm (3ft)	Either	0.6-1.2m (2-4ft)	**Formal** once: summer **Informal** once: after flowering
Buxus sempervirens (Box)	Evergreen	1-2m (4ft)	Either	1.2m (4ft)	Twice: late spring and early autumn Once: late summer
Carpinus betulus (Hornbeam)	Deciduous	60cm (2ft)	Formal	1.5-6m (5-20ft)	
Chamaecyparis lawsoniana (Lawson's cypress)	Evergreen	1.2m (4ft)	Formal	1.2-2.4m (4-8ft)	Twice: late spring and early autumn
Cotoneaster lacteus (Cotoneaster)	Evergreen	90cm (3ft)	Informal	1.5-2.2m (5-7ft)	Once: after fruiting
Crataegus monogyna (Hawthorn)	Deciduous	60cm (2ft)	Either	1.5-3m (5-10ft)	**Formal** twice: summer and autumn **Informal** once: in winter
Elaeagnus x ebbingei	Evergreen	1.2m (4ft)	Formal	1.5-3m (5-10ft)	Once: mid to late summer
Escallonia spp	Evergreen	90cm (3ft)	Either	1.2-2.4m (4-8ft)	Once: immediately after flowering
Fagus sylvatica (Beech)	Deciduous	60cm (2ft)	Formal	1.5-6m (5-20ft)	Once: late summer
Fuchsia magellanica	Deciduous	60cm (2ft)	Informal	1-1.5m (3-5ft)	Once: spring to remove old stems
Ilex aquifolium (Holly)	Evergreen	90cm (3ft)	Either	2-4m (6½-13ft)	Once: late summer For berries: once, in early spring
Lavandula spp (Lavender)	Evergreen	30cm (1ft)	Either	0.5-1m (1½-3ft)	Twice: spring and after flowering
Ligustrum spp (Privet)	Evergreen	45cm (1½ft)	Formal	1.5-6m (5-20ft)	Three times; not in winter
Prunus laurocerasus (Laurel)	Evergreen	75cm (2½ft)	Formal	1.2-3m (4-10ft)	Once: mid to late summer
Pyracantha (Firethorn)	Evergreen	75cm (2½ft)	Either	2-3m (6½-10ft)	Twice: after flowering and in autumn (avoid berries)
Rosa rugosa	Deciduous	90cm (3ft)	Informal	1-1.5m (3-5ft)	Once: in spring, remove oldest
Taxus baccata (Yew)	Evergreen	60cm (2ft)	Formal	1.2-6m (4-20ft)	Twice: summer and autumn
Viburnum tinus	Evergreen	60cm (2ft)	Informal	1-2.4m (3-8ft)	Once: after flowering

Topiary

Topiary is a form of pruning, training and clipping plants into artificial shapes. The designs can be elaborate or simple, and have a strong architectural element. As well as being suited to hedges and plants in containers, topiary in the garden makes a strong focal point, adding to the structural and vertical interest.

The more intricate the shape, the more frequently the pruning and training has to be done. The secret with topiary is little and often. Trim shoots while they are short, to keep them branching. This is best done by pinching out the growing point between finger and thumb. Most designs are easy to form, if you create a template or framework to help avoid uneven trimming. The plants most suited to topiary are small-leaved, slow-growing evergreens, as they retain their shape and require less frequent clipping. Box (*Buxus sempervirens*) and yew (*Taxus buccata*) are among the most popular shrubs for this purpose. A quick-growing, poor man's topiary centre can be created by training a climber like ivy (*Hedera helix*) over a topiary frame.

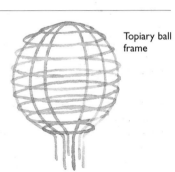

Topiary cone
Box is grown into a striking topiary cone (left), adding structure to a perennial border.

Paired topiary
Round box topiary (above) is paired to elegant effect to focus attention on a weathered statue.

Shaping simple topiary

For the beginner, a simple uncomplicated shape is ideal, because topiary requires a fair degree of precision, and techniques which are slightly different than those used for many other forms of pruning. All of the cutting tools used for clipping topiary must be extremely sharp because the shoots are very soft and sappy when pruned and prone to disease if torn.

It is easy to forget that training topiary is a combination of tying shoots into position as well as pruning and trimming.

Training a pyramid
1 *When the shrub is roughly 45cm (18in) tall, create a cone-shaped frame using three canes.*

2 *Pinch out the top growing point so lateral shoots develop, and clip shoots outside the frame.*

Topiary forms

The more elaborate the intended topiary figure, the longer it will take to create, with figures of birds and animals taking years of skill and patience to achieve a recognizable outline and shape.

Basic designs and forms take in cones, globes, obelisks and pyramids, with spirals being introduced into these basic shapes.

To make clipping and shaping more symmetrical, frames or templates (either ready-made or simply constructed from wires or canes) can be used as a guide, with the frame being lowered over the selected plant, and the plant being trimmed to shape as it grows through the frame (see left).

The frame can be left in position to provide structural support throughout the year.

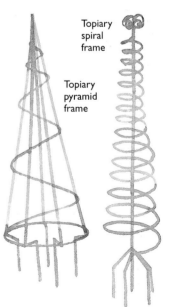

Topiary ball frame

Topiary spiral frame

Topiary pyramid frame

Plants for particular purposes

The following plants are valuable for particular situations. Some are ideal for planting in hanging baskets or containers, others, such as trees and evergreen shrubs, make especially useful framework plants for the garden.

A range of choices for perennial borders are listed according to colour, and there are also suggestions for plants with interesting foliage colour to add to mixed shrub and perennial plantings.

Key

a = annual and biennial
a/p tender perennials treated as annuals
b = bulb
c = climber
p = perennial
s = shrub
t = tree

Good container plants

Agapanthus (p – blue)
Ageratum (a – blue)
Alonsoa (a – orange)
Argyranthemum (a/p – white, pink, yellow)
Begonia semperflorens (a – mixed colours)
Begonia x *tuberhybrida* (a/p - pink, red, orange, white)
Bidens ferulifolia (a – yellow)
Brachyscome iberidifolia (a – blue)
Buxus sempervirens (s – foliage)
Cordyline australis (p – foliage)
Diascia (p – pink, orange)
Felicia amelloides (a – blue)
Fuchsia (s – pink, purple, red)
Helichrysum petiolare (a/p – foliage)
Hosta (p – foliage)
Hyacinthus (b – mixed colours)
Hydrangea (s – blue, pink, white)
Impatiens walleriana (a/p – white, pink, red)
Laurus nobilis (s – foliage)
Lobelia (a – blue, pink, white)
Narcissus (b – yellow, white)
Nemisia (a – mixed colours)
Pelargonium (a/p – orange, pink, red, white)
Petunia (a/p – mixed colours)
Phormium (p - foliage)
Primula (p – mixed colours)
Senecio cinerea (a/p – foliage)
Tagetes (a – yellow, orange)
Tropaeolum (a – red, orange, yellow)
Tulipa (b – mixed colours)
Verbena x *hybrida* (a/p – mixed colours)
Viola x *wittrockiana* (a – mixed colours)

Good hanging basket plants

Ageratum (a – blue)
Alonsoa (a – orange)
Argyranthemum (a/p – white, pink, yellow)
Begonia semperflorens (a – mixed colours)
Begonia x *tuberhybrida* (a/p - pink, red, orange, white)
Bidens ferulifolia (a – yellow)
Brachyscome iberidifolia (a – blue)
Diascia (p – pink, orange)
Felicia amelloides (a – blue)
Fuchsia (s – pink, purple, red)
Glechoma hederacea 'Variegata' (a – foliage)
Hedera helix (p – foliage)
Helichrysum petiolare (a/p – foliage)
Impatiens walleriana (a– white, pink, red)
Lobelia erinus (a –blue, pink, white)
Lotus berthelottii (p – orange, foliage)
Narcissus (b – yellow, white)
Pelargonium (a/p – orange, pink, red, white)
Petunia (a/p – mixed colours)
Plectranthus coleoides (a/p – foliage)
Primula (p – mixed colours)
Scaevola (a/p – purple, blue)
Senecio cinerea (a/p – foliage)
Tagetes (a – yellow, orange)
Tropaeolum (a – red, orange, yellow)
Tulipa (b – mixed colours)
Verbena x *hybrida* (a/p – mixed colours)
Viola x *wittrockiana* (a – mixed colours)

Perennial plants for colour

Blue/mauve flowers

Aconitum spp. and cvs
Agapanthus spp. and cvs
Ajuga reptans
Anchusa azurea
Aquilegia flabellata
Aster amellus
Aster x *frikartii*
Baptisia australis
Brunnera macrophylla
Campanula spp. and cvs
Catananche caerulea
Delphinium hybrids
Echinops ritro
Eryngium spp. and cvs
Galega officinalis
Gentiana spp. and cvs
Geranium spp. and cvs
Hosta spp. and cvs
Iris spp. and cvs
Limonium platyphyllum
Linum narbonense
Lithodora diffusa
Meconopsis spp.
Nepeta spp. and cvs
Omphalodes cappadocica
Penstemon heterophyllus
Perovskia atriplicifolia
Platycodon grandoflorus
Polemonium caeruleum
Primula spp. and cvs
Pulmonaria spp. and cvs.
Salvia spp. and cvs.
Scabiosa caucasica
Tradescantia x *andersoniana*
Verbena rigida
Veronica spp. and cvs

Yellow, gold and orange flowers

Achillea spp. and cvs
Aurinia saxatilis
Anthemis tinctoria
Asphodeline lutea
Bupthalmum salicifolium
Centaurea macrocephalum
Cephalaria gigantea
Coreopsis verticillata
Digitalis lutea
Euphorbia spp. and cvs
Geum 'Lady Strathenden'
Helenium spp. and cvs
Helianthus spp. and cvs
Heliopsis spp. and cvs
Hemerocallis spp. and cvs
Hieracium spp. and cvs
Inula spp. and cvs
Iris pseudacorus
Kniphofia 'Little Maid'
Ligularia spp. and cvs
Lysimachia punctata
Lysimachia nummularia 'Aurea'
Oenothera spp. and cvs.
Paeonia mlokosewitschii
Potentilla recta
Primula spp. and cvs
Ranunculus spp. and cvs
Rudbeckia spp. and cvs
Solidago spp. and cvs
Thalictrum flavum spp. *glaucum*
Trollius spp. and cvs
Verbascum spp. and cvs

Red flowers

Achillea 'Cerise Queen'
Alcea rosea
Astilbe 'Fanal'
Astrantia major 'Ruby Wedding'
Centranthus ruber
Cosmos atrosanguineus
Dianthus 'Brympton Red'
Geum 'Mrs Bradshaw'
Hemerocallis 'Stafford'
Lobelia 'Cherry Ripe'
Lupinus 'Inverewe Red'
Lychnis chaceldonica
Monarda didyma 'Cambridge Scarlet'
Paeonia spp. and cvs
Papaver orientale
Penstemon 'Cherry Ripe'
Persicaria amplexicaulis
Potentilla 'Gibson's Scarlet'

Pink flowers

Anemone x *hybrida*
Armeria spp. and cvs
Aster spp. and cvs
Astilbe spp. and cvs
Bergenia cordifolia
Dianthus spp. and cvs
Diascia spp. and cvs
Dicentra spp. and cvs
Erigeron 'Charity'

Erodioum manescauii
Filipendula spp. and cvs
Geranium spp. and cvs
Lamium roseum
Linaria purpurea 'Cannon Went'
Lychnis flos-jovis
Lythrum spp. and cvs
Malva moschata
Monarda didyma 'Croftway Pink'
Papaver orientale 'Cedric Morris'
Penstemon 'Hidcote Pink'
Persicaria spp. and cvs
Phlox paniculata cvs
Phuopsis stylosa
Primula spp. and cvs
Sedum spectabile
Sidalcea spp. and cvs

Purple flowers

Aster spp. and cvs
Centaurea spp. and cvs
Echinacea purpurea
Erigeron 'Dunkelste Aller'
Erysimum 'Bowles Mauve'
Geranium spp. and cvs
Liatris spicata
Linaria purpurea
Lythrum spp. and cvs
Osteospermum jucundum
Penstemon 'Burgundy'
Phlox 'Le Mahdi'
Senecio pulcher
Stachys macrantha
Thalictrum delavayi
Verbena bonariensis

White flowers

Achillea ptarmica 'The Pearl'
Anaphalis margaritacea
Anemone x hybrida 'Honorine Jobert'
Anthemis punctata cupaniana
Argyranthemum frutescens
Aruncus dioicus
Astilbe 'Irrlicht'
Campanula latiloba alba
Crambe cordifolia
Dianthus 'Haytor White'
Dictamnus albus
Echinops sphaerocephalus
Geranium sanguineum 'Album'
Gypsophila paniculata 'Bristol Fairy'
Hosta spp. and cvs
Lamium maculatum 'White Nancy'
Leucanthemum 'Everest'
Lysimachia clethroides
Osteospermum 'Whirligig'
Phlox 'Fujiama'

Physostegia virginiana 'Alba'
Polygonatum x hybridum
Pulmonaria 'Sissinghurst White'
Romneya coulteri
Smilacina racemosa
Trillum grandiflorum
Yucca spp.

Foliage colour
Silver foliage

Artemisia spp. and cvs (p)
Cerastium tomentosum (p)
Convolvulus cneorum (s)
Cynara cardunculus (p)
Elaeagnus 'Quicksilver' (s)
Eryngium giganteum (p)
Hebe pingifolia 'Pagei' (s)
Lavandula angustifolia (s)
Melianthus major (a/p)
Onopordum spp. (a)
Pyrus salicifolia 'Pendula' (t)
Santolina chamaecyparis (p)
Senecio cineraria (a/p)
Stachys byzantina (p)
Tanacetum haradjanii (p)

Purple foliage

Acer palmatum 'Atropurpureum' (t)
Ajuga reptans 'Atropurpurea' (p)
Berberis thunbergii 'Atropurpurea' (s)
Clematis recta 'Purpurea' (p)
Cordyline australis 'Atropurpurea' (p)
Corylus maxima 'Purpurea' (s)
Cotinus coggygria 'Royal Purple' (s)
Dahlia 'Bishop of Llandaff' (p)
Fagus sylvatica 'Riversii' (t)
Foeniculum vulgare 'Purpureum' (p)
Heuchera micrantha 'Purple Purple' (p)
Lobelia cardinalis (p)
Phormium tenax 'Purpureum' (p)
Prunus cerasifera 'Nigra' (t)
Ricinus communis 'Gibsonii' (a)
Rosa glauca (s)
Salvia officinalis 'Purpurascens' (s)
Sedum maximum atropurpureum (p)
Viola riviniana Purpurea Group (p)
Vitis vinifera 'Purpurea' (c)

Golden foliage

Acer japonicum 'Aurea' (t)
Carex stricta 'Bowles Golden' (p)

Filipendula ulmaria 'Aurea' (p)
Fuchsia 'Golden Treasure' (s)
Gleditsia triacanthos 'Sunburst' (t)
Hebe armstrongii (s)
Hedera helix 'Buttercup' (c)
Hosta spp. and cvs (p)
Humulus lupulus 'Aureus' (c)
Ligustrum ovalifolium 'Aureum' (s)
Lonicera nitida 'Baggesen's Gold' (s)
Lysimachia nummularia 'Aurea' (p)
Milium effusum 'Aureum' (p)
Oreganum vulgare 'Aureum' (p)
Philadelphus coronarius 'Aureus' (s)
Physocarpus opulifolius 'Luteus' (s)
Robinia pseudoacacia 'Frisia' (t)
Sambucus racemosa 'Plumosa Aurea' (s)
Tanecetum parthenium 'Aureum' (p)
Taxus baccata 'Aurea' (t)

Blue foliage

Elymus magellanicus (p)
Hosta 'Halcyon' (p)
Hosta sieboldiana 'Elegans' (p)

Variegated foliage

Acer negundo 'Variegatum' (t)
Aktinidia kolomikta (s)
Aquilegia vulgaris 'Woodside' (p)
Aralia elata 'Aureovariegata' (t)
Astrantia major 'Sunningdale Variegated' (p)
Brunnera macrophylla 'Hadspen Cream' (p)
Cornus alba 'Elegantissima' (s)
Cortaderia selloana 'Gold Band' (p)
Elaeagnus pungens 'Maculata' (s)
Eryngium bourgatii (p)
Euonymus fortunei 'Emerald 'n' Gold' (s)
Euphorbia marginata (a)
Fragaria x ananassa 'Variegata' (p)
Hakonechloa macra 'Aureola' (p)
Hedera spp. and cvs (c)
Hosta spp. and cvs (p)
Ilex spp. and cvs (t)
Iris pallida 'Variegata' (p)
Lamium maculatum (p)
Lonicera japonica 'Aureo-reticulata' (c)
Miscanthus sinensis 'Zebrinus' (p)
Phalaris arunindinacea 'Picta' (p)
Phormium tenax 'Sundowner' (p)
Pleioblastus auricomus (p)

Pulmonaria saccharata (p)
Rhamnus alaternus 'Argenteovariegata' (t)
Salvia officinalis 'Icterina' (s)
Silybum marianum (a)
Sisyrinchium striatum 'Aunt May' (p)
Symphytum x uplandicum 'Variegatum' (p)
Tanecetum vulgare 'Silver Lace' (p)
Vinca major 'Variegata' (s)

Small trees

Acer griseum
Betula pendula 'Youngii'
Cercis siliquastrum
Ilex x altaclarensis
Laburnum x waterei 'Vosii'
Malus 'Profusion'
Prunus serrula
Pyrus salicifolia 'Pendula'
Sorbus hupehensis

Evergreen shrubs

Abelia spp. and cvs
Azara spp.
Berberis spp. and cvs
Buxus sempervirens
Ceanothus spp. and cvs
Choisya ternata
Convolvulus cneorum
Cotoneaster spp. and cvs
Daphne spp. and cvs
Elaeagnus pungens
Escalonia spp. and cvs
Euonymus fortunei
Garrya elliptica
Hebe spp. and cvs
Ilex spp. and cvs
Laurus nobilis
Mahonia spp. and cvs
Osmanthus spp. and cvs
Photinia spp. and cvs
Pieris spp. and cvs
Prunus lusitanicus
Rhododendron spp. and cvs
Sarcococca spp. and cvs
Skimmia japonica
Viburnum tinus
Vinca spp. and cvs

Index

Acknowledgements

The photographer, publishers and authors would like to thank the following people and organizations who kindly allowed us to photograph their gardens:

Ansells Garden Centre, Horningsea, Cambs; David Austin Roses Ltd, Wolverhampton, West Midlands; Bressingham Gardens, Diss, Norfolk; Broadlands Garden, Hazelbury Bryan, Dorset; Cambridge Alpines, Cottenham, Cambs; Cambridge Garden Plants, Horningsea, Cambs; Capel Manor, Enfield, Middx; Beth Chatto Gardens, Elmstead Market, Essex; Clare College, Cambridge, Cambs; Docwras Manor, Shepreth, Cambs; John Drake, Fen Ditton, Cambs; Mrs Sally Edwards, Horningsea, Cambs; Peter Elliott, Hauxton, Cambs; Mr and Mrs R. Foulser, Cerne Abbas, Dorset; Holkham Garden Centre, Holkham, Norfolk; Kiftsgate Court Gardens, Chipping Campden, Gloucs; Joy Larkcom, Hepworth, Norfolk; Madingley Hall Gardens, Madingley, Cambs; The Manor, Herningford Grey, Cambs; Paradise Centre, Lamarsh, Suffolk; Royal Horticultural Society's Gardens, Wisley, Surrey; Royal National Rose Society, St. Albans, Herts; Scotsdales Garden Centre, Shelford, Cambs; Trevor Scott, Thorpe-le-Soken, Essex; Scarlett's Plants, West Bergholt, Essex; Mr and Mrs M. Stuart-Smith, Cambridge, Cambs; Anthony Surtees, Crondall, Hampshire; University Botanic Gardens, Cambridge, Cambs; Unwins Seeds Ltd, Histon, Cambs; John Wingate and the Golders Green Allotment Association; Wyken Hall, Stanton, Suffolk; Patricia Zaphros, Fen Ditton, Cambs.

The publishers are also grateful to the following for their help and support in the production of this book:

Phoebus Editions Ltd for conceptual work on the Care and Maintenance section; Paul Draycott, Roger Sygrave and the staff of Capel Manor; the staff of RHS Wisley; David Raeburn, John Wingate and the members of the Golders Green Allotment Association; Andrew Lord and the staff of The Garden Picture Library, London SW11.

Suppliers of containers, plants, tools and equipment:

Chiltern Seeds, Ulverston, Cumbria; Granville Garden Centre, London NW2; Squires Garden Centre, Twickenham, Middx.

Picture credits:
(Key: R–Right, L–Left, T–Top, M–Middle, C–Centre, B–Bottom)

Designing the Garden, **p.6–p.65:**
All pictures by The Garden Picture Library except: *The Complete Guide to Gardening with Containers* (Collins & Brown, 1995): p.7 (TL inset); p.52 (BL, B C); p.53 (BL, B C). Michelle Garrett: p.52 (BR); p.62 (BL). George Taylor: p.28 (CR, BL, BR); p.29 (CL, CM, CR, BL, BM, BR); p.30 (CL, CM, CR, BL, BR); p.31 (all); p.32 (CL, CM, CM inset, CR, BL); p.33 (CL, CR, BL, BM, BR); p.34 (2nd row L, R, 3rd row L, M, BL, BM); p.35 (CL, CM, CR, BL, BM, BR); p.38 (CL, CM, CR, BL, BM, BR); p.44 (BC, BR, BR inset); p.45 (all); p.47 (BL, BR); p.49 (all); p.51 (TL, TCL, TCR, TR, BL); p.58 (CL, CR, BL, BM, BR).

Care and Maintenance, **p.66–p.125:**
All photographs by George Taylor except: A-Z Botanical Collections Ltd: p.105 (BR). *The Complete Guide to Gardening with Containers* (Collins & Brown, 1995): p.67 (TL inset); p.81 (BL); p.83 (TL, TM, TR, BM); p.88 (BR); p.92 (BC). The Garden Picture Library: p.68 (TR); p.69 (BR); p.77 (TL, BL); p.79 (TR); p.80 (BL); p.83 (BR); p.86 (TR); p.88 (TR); p.90 (TR, BL); p.91 (2nd row R); p.92 (TR); p.97 (TL); p.102 (TR); p.103 (B 2nd L, B 2nd R); p.104 (BL); p.105 (TL, T 2nd L, TR, BL); p.106 (TR); p.108 (TR); p.110 (TR); p.114 (TR); p.118 (TR); p.119 (TR); p.120 (TR); p.123 (TL, TR); p.124 (TR). *Gardening with Herbs* (Jacqui Hurst for Collins & Brown, 1996): p.80 (TR, BR). Holt Studios International: p.103 (TL, T 2nd L, T 2nd R, TR, BR); p.104 (T 2nd L, T 2nd R, TR, B 2nd L, B 2nd R, BR); p.105 (T 2nd R, B 2nd R). Sam Lloyd: p.81 (BL); p.83 (TM). Peter McHoy: p.103 (BL); p.104 (TL); p.105 (B 2nd L). Howard Rice: p.74 (BL, BR); p.75 (BL, BR); p.110 (BL, B 2nd L, B 2nd R, BR); p.117 (BL, BM, BR).